SMALL MOVES
Big Gains

Teacher habits

THAT HELP KIDS TO

✓ Talk More

✓ Think More

✓ Achieve More

NANCY MOTLEY

Published by Seidlitz Education
P.O. Box 166827
Irving, TX 75016
www.seidlitzeducation.com

For related titles and support materials visit www.seidlitzeducation.com.

3.23

contents

Turning *Small Moves* into *Habits*

Small moves: we all make them. They are the tiny little decisions that propel us through our day.

Let's take a look at my morning, I got out of bed after hitting snooze only once. This is two less "snoozes" than my norm (because my husband was snoring and I knew I wouldn't get back to sleep). After brushing my teeth I decided to throw on a sweatshirt over my PJs instead of getting dressed in the workout clothes I had laid out. Next I woke up my daughter for school. When she didn't immediately stir, I lay down next to her for a couple of minutes and softly brushed the hair off of her face. Once she opened her eyes, I went to her closet, picked out her clothes for the day, and then headed downstairs. After starting the coffee, I grabbed my phone and began scrolling through Facebook.

In these first 15 minutes of my day, how many small moves did I make? A bunch. Many of them were mindless, requiring no thought on my part because I make them every day. Hitting snooze, brushing my teeth, waking Caroline, picking out her clothes, starting coffee, and scrolling Facebook are all part of what I would call my morning routine. For better or worse, those are all things I do almost every single morning without any deliberate thought.

I also made a few small moves this particular morning that were not part of my everyday routine; namely, only snoozing once, putting on my sweatshirt, and snuggling with my daughter for a few minutes. In each of these tiny moments, a thought prompted me to stray from my routine.

Just like my automatic small moves, these seemingly inconsequential decisions had an impact on both me and my family. Because I got out of bed 20 minutes earlier, I felt less rushed to get everyone out the door. Because I never got out of my PJs, I dramatically decreased the likelihood that I would work out. Because I lay with Caroline for a few minutes, my normally grumpy middle schooler was pleasant when she came downstairs.

So what does my morning routine have to do with you and your students? On the surface not much, but when we dig a little deeper, we can see that it actually has everything to do with what goes on in your classroom.

We make small moves every minute of teaching. Some of these tiny, seemingly inconsequential decisions are automatic and habitual, while others are made in response to a particular situation or student. Additionally, each of these small moves has an impact on our students; some positive, some negative. Sometimes the result is dramatic change, and other times the result of our small moves is undetectable. These moments, these tiny decision points, these indetectable actions, and these minor moves toward a different outcome are the focus of this book. Rather than offering a gigantic framework for success or a long-term plan for systemic change, what I offer are simply some small moves … 23, to be exact.

What Is A Small Move?

Well ... a small move is the opposite of a big move. Big moves require a lot of effort. Small moves require only a little effort. Big change feels really hard. Small change feels possible. Big plans are usually complicated. Small plans are simple.

Merriam-Webster defines a "move" as "a step taken especially to gain an objective." A quick Google search yielded this slightly different definition: "an action that initiates or advances a process or plan." When we think in terms of education, our objectives, our processes, and our plans all center around students becoming successful. I think we can all agree that our common goal is to help students achieve their full potential with regard to their content knowledge, communication skills, and ability to think critically. A move is anything we do to advance toward that goal. So what is a "small move"?

In order for any idea to make it into this book, it had to pass the "small move" test. That is to say, the idea, the habit, the hack, or the technique had to be a move toward our common goal as mentioned above, and it also had to be small.

More specifically, the moves had to meet the following criteria:

1. **Benefit all learners.** Most of my professional career has been focused on meeting the needs of English learners. The content of this book definitely supports students who are learning English, but it will also support students living in poverty, students in need of special modifications and/or accommodations, students who are disengaged, and even students who are already excelling.

2. **Require low/no preparation.** Teachers have very little prep time, and the little we have is often taken up with meetings and administrative tasks. We all need to be able to try out a new idea without a huge time investment.

3. **Be actionable.** Can a teacher take each idea and go do it? I want the move to be small enough that teachers can jump in with both feet and give it a go.

4. **Apply to all content areas.** Whether you are a self-contained PreK teacher like Ms. Mercado in Spring Branch ISD or an Advanced Algebra 2 teacher like Mrs. Dismukes at Brenham High School, you can use these moves. I'll highlight variations of each small move as needed to account for differences in age and/or content.

5. **Be brief.** Some of the small moves can be made in one to two minutes during class, and others literally take no instructional time at all. A previous working title for some of my ideas was "60 Second Solutions," and while the content has evolved, the ideas are all still quick.

Why Focus on Small Moves?

For the past 10 years, I have trained hundreds of groups of teachers on a wide variety of instructional techniques. During each face-to-face (F2F) or virtual training, I model strategies first, then we break down each component together and identify ways to troubleshoot challenges. I often give participants time to plan for their own classrooms, and they leave energized and excited to "turn around" these ideas while I leave confident that I've equipped them with new ways to help their students.

I also get the opportunity to follow up with many of the teachers who attend a training by observing them while they teach their students. Following these observations, I provide individual and small group feedback. It was during these coaching sessions that I realized the need for a focus on small moves. Time and again, my feedback to them did not encourage a complete overhaul of a teacher's lesson, but rather a tweak to a component of the lesson. A small move. I might say something like, "I noticed after you gave directions for the partner conversations that most partnerships came up with one answer and then got off task. Next time, try encouraging them to give at least three different answers to your question. This usually prompts better partner discussions." (For details on this small move, see *Pick a Number* on p. 49.) In this example, the teacher leaves our conversation ready and able to make an adjustment immediately. That small tweak to the way he/she gives directions can have a big impact on the quality of the students' conversations.

Small moves can be the fastest and easiest path toward positive change. Doing something little and simple is palatable. A tiny change feels doable. Think about the difference in these two requests that you might hear from your principal at a staff meeting:

> **Request #1:** *Ok guys, we have a new lesson planning template. Here is what it looks like. We made this change because we are shifting toward being more focused on developing our students' academic language, and we want the plans to reflect that. Notice there are several places for you to incorporate sentence stems throughout the lesson. Be sure to include the language objective in the box at the top. Don't forget to fill in all of the other 11 sections for each lesson as well. Starting next week, I'll expect each of you to use this in lieu of your current format. (Insert deadpan stare)*

> **Request #2:** *After looking at our data, we realize we need to shift toward being more focused on developing our students' academic language. We want your lesson plans to reflect that. Our first step will be to include a sentence stem for each lesson. Here are some examples of what I am looking for.*

In request #1, your principal asks you to make the huge change of completely overhauling the way you write your lessons. In request #2, the change is much smaller: adding a sentence stem to each plan. Which one feels more doable? Which one would you have more inclination to follow? Request #2 of course! When the move is small, we can take action quickly with a clearly defined purpose. When the move requires extended thought and planning, it is easy to become overwhelmed with where to start, which direction to follow, and how to find the time to execute.

Some might wonder if I am oversimplifying everything. What I am suggesting — that small moves can translate into big gains for students — might sound a little gimmicky, like the infomercials you watch late at night: "Flawless skin in three easy steps," "Low calorie meals in just ten minutes," "Never miss a perfect night's sleep again." You might be thinking, "Come on, of course you can't fix all the challenges I face in the classroom with small moves," or "How on earth can a few 'tiny decisions' really help all my students become successful?" Of course, serious obstacles need serious solutions, which means we are forever in search of strategies and ideas that will help our students be more engaged, more successful, and more confident.

Here's the thing, though: all of us have already attended trainings or read books where we learned strategies and ideas that will help. I have bookshelves full of awesome resources that offer ways for me to become a better teacher. I have watched countless webinars and participated in online trainings with some of the most expert educators around. The problem is that even though I am a "true believer" in those sessions, my actual implementation of the techniques usually pales in comparison. Why is that? Simply because often the ideas require a significant amount

of planning to put into practice. Sometimes, because the presenter made it look so easy, I try it immediately but end up with more questions than answers. Another problem with implementation is that I have to practice "live" during instructional time. What if I try a new lesson and it bombs? Then I am an entire day behind on the pacing guide — the one that leaves no room for mistakes. For these reasons, it is easy to enter into "implementation stagnation," which is how I refer to the pitfall of never actually using new techniques (even though we really like them) or only trying out a small portion of strategies we learn.

Starting small mitigates implementation stagnation. When I choose one small move, I do not have to devote a lot of time to planning. Each small move has a singular focus, so the goal is uncomplicated and direct. Also, the cost of trying it out live is minimal because I can still deliver my lesson as planned, even if the small move doesn't seem to work as I had hoped.

Will any of these small moves solve every classroom problem? Of course not. Will implementing all of the small moves in this book be enough to transform every student into a superstar valedictorian? No, but what every single small move will do is allow you to take action. When you make these moves, you are increasing your students' abilities to think critically and communicate effectively one small step at a time. And ultimately, when you make these moves your everyday habits, you will see your students not only think more and talk more, but they will undoubtedly achieve more.

What Is a Habit?

My favorite definition of a habit is "a regular practice," especially one that is hard to give up. Putting on my seatbelt before I put my car in drive and checking my phone when I hear a "ding" for a text message are two examples that come to mind. Both are hard for me not to do; they are habits. We all have habits, both in our personal lives and in our professional lives. Think about your current habits in your classroom. Do you always greet your students at the door? Do you have a routine for how and when you grade assignments? What comes to mind when you find yourself saying, "Well that is the way I've always done that"? All of us probably have a habit for how to start class, for example. You begin in the exact same way each day. As you read through this book, I encourage you to regularly reflect on your own habits as a teacher. Without a doubt your current habits impact your students' achievement, sometimes positively and possibly sometimes negatively. It is important to note that each of those habits almost certainly began as a small move. This is why small moves are so profound. The goal is to make the most effective small moves we can and then to focus on making those moves habits (i.e., regular practices that are hard to give up).

Ultimately, when you make these moves your everyday habits, you will see your students not only think more and talk more, but they will undoubtedly achieve more.

How Do Habits Work?

Let's begin by developing our understanding of habits. The teacher in me knows the value of building background and activating prior knowledge at the beginning of new learning, so that is what we will do here. The good news for us is that there is quite a bit of research and information out there about habits and how to create them (or, in the case of bad ones, how to break them).

The process of forming a habit is often described as a "habit loop" with three steps: cue, routine, and reward (Duhigg, 2014, p. 19). The cue triggers your brain to perform the routine (habit), which will result in the desired reward.

For example: Waking up with bad breath (**cue**) triggers you to go brush your teeth (**routine**) which makes your breath fresh (**reward**).

The same habit loop occurs over and over again in our classrooms as well. When the bell rings at 9:10 a.m. (cue), you take attendance (routine) so the front office doesn't call you over the intercom, interrupting instruction (reward). Gabriel is incessantly tapping his pencil (cue), so you walk over and gently touch his pencil, making eye contact with him (routine), and he stops tapping ... for now (reward). Several students look confused as you explain the meaning of a new term (cue), so you explain it in a different way (routine), causing their faces to "unwrinkle" (reward).

Another slightly different way to think about a habit is as a four-step process: cue, craving, routine/response, and reward (Clear, 2018). The only change here is the addition of "craving." The idea is that no matter what the cues are, each person has to crave the reward enough to take action. In the previous examples, there are teachers who might not crave the reward enough to execute the routine.

Pencil tapping might not bother them; when they see confusion, some teachers might proceed with the original explanation, thinking that students will understand once they get through all of it; and for the attendance example, I can assure you that the front office team knows exactly who does not crave uninterrupted instruction because they have to call those teachers almost daily.

Here are a few more examples of how the habit loop might look in a classroom setting:

CUE	CRAVING	RESPONSE	REWARD
Students are getting too loud	I want a quiet classroom	Turn off the lights	Students get quieter
Students are working silently	I want something to do while they work to get rid of the feeling that I am not "doing my job"	Walk the room and look over their shoulders to monitor their work	Feel like I am "doing my job"
Marcela is off task again	I want her to stay focused	Ask her to come sit at my small group table to finish her work	Marcela moves and gets started on the next question on her assignment
Some students don't have their cameras on during the Zoom lesson	I want to make sure everyone is paying attention	Ask students to type agree or disagree with the question in the chat	I can see that the five students who aren't showing video gave a response in the chat

Where Do I Begin With Changing My Teaching Habits?

Sometimes a teacher will ask me to sign their copy of my previous book, *Talk, Read, Talk, Write*. When that happens, I always write this short note: **Be Intentional**. My goal as a teacher is to be thoughtful about each decision I make. This two-word phrase drives me: be intentional. I'm always thinking about ways to be more intentional. For example, my thoughts include these questions:

- **What writing opportunities are my kids getting in this lesson?**

- **Which visual support should I use?**

- **How many practice items are the right amount?**

- **Is there a student who needs a little extra support from me today?**

- **What is the best way to word this definition so that my students will really grasp it?**

I don't always succeed, but being intentional is always my challenge to myself and to other teachers.

In his book, *Atomic Habits*, James Clear (2018) provides a simple road map for me, and I would argue for all teachers, to achieve our professional goals: "1. Decide the type of person you want to be, and 2. Prove it to yourself with small wins" (p. 39). In other words, decide the type of teacher you want to be, and prove it to yourself by making small moves that show it. In my case, I want to be an intentional teacher, so I make the small moves to plan writing opportunities, to find effective visuals, to quantify the number of practice items, and to select specific students for focus.

What type of teacher do you want to be? Pause and think about it. Forget all the challenges, let go of any limitations you see, and ask yourself, *What type of teacher do I want to be?* Thinking about your answer to that question also begs another question: Does the type of teacher you want to be align with the type of teacher you actually are? If reflecting on your teacher identity isn't something you've spent very much time doing, don't worry. If your answers to both of the above questions are, "I have no clue," fear not. There are two highly reliable sources of information to help you determine the type of teacher you are: your students and your colleagues. They know the type of teacher you are by the moves you make.

Take Ms. Brown, my daughter's seventh grade science teacher. Audrey tells me all the time that Ms. Brown is "really nice" and "totally gets us." The only way Audrey formed this opinion is through experiencing Ms. Brown's small moves — her habits. What Ms. Brown does everyday demonstrates that. Audrey will tell you that Ms. Brown always has music ("that we actually like") playing when they enter her room each period. She also writes short, little, heartfelt notes to students and puts them on their desks. Each week whenever she is reviewing material, she wears a silly hat backward, walks backward, and sometimes wears her clothes backward to "recap" content. She opens her classroom every Thursday during her lunch for students to eat with her. Ms. Brown obviously cares about making a connection with her students and wants to be the type of teacher who has solid relationships with them. Her small moves reflect that.

What will the small moves in this book reflect? I put it in the subtitle of the book: *Teacher Habits That Help Kids to Think More, Talk More, and Achieve More*. This book will help you to become the type of teacher whose students think critically, communicate effectively, and achieve success as measured in any given discipline. In the chart to the right, the small moves are grouped to support those goals. It is also how the remaining chapters are divided.

How do you begin to improve your teacher habits? Decide what type of teacher you want to become, and make a small move to show it.

As you read through the remaining chapters to learn about the 23 small moves (see chart), I can imagine that many of the ideas will seem familiar to you. You may read the small move *Smile* on p. 65 and think to yourself, "Seriously? Smiling in front of my students?? Does she think I don't know that?!" Or when you read about using a timer on p. 78, you might think, "Oh good, I already do that. I always set a timer for their warm-ups." Like I mentioned before, none of these moves are Earth-shattering. None of them are all that difficult, and many might be techniques you are already implementing. The challenge is transforming each of those small moves into automatic habits. We all know we need to smile, but is it habitual? It is easy to smile first thing in the morning, especially if you have a student who walks in excited to see

TYPE OF TEACHER	SMALL MOVES
I want to be the type of teacher whose students can speak effectively in an academic setting. *Talk More*	• Package and Parrot • Target the Talk • Prove It (a.k.a. Because…) • Appointed Roles • Anyone's Idea • Prep the Speaker • Plus Minus
I want to be the type of teacher whose students think critically. *Think More*	• Stop Fishing • Pronounce, Predict, Paraphrase • Pick a Number • Set a Purpose • Listen For … • Solo Sandwich • Accurate Answer • Non-Example
I want to be the type of teacher whose students learn content deeply. *Achieve More*	• Smile • Public Success • Color-Code • Touch to Teach • Tell a Story • Timer • Fewest Words Possible • Walk With Intention

you, but are you smiling at 2:00 p.m. on Thursday when you are recording yourself giving directions for a virtual lesson for the 3rd time? So you use a timer for every warm-up. That's great! Do you use a timer when you ask students to talk at their tables? What about when they are completing independent assignments? How about on early release days? In other words, are smiling and using a timer habitual? The goal of this book is to make each of these small moves habits.

Why Is it Important to Focus on Turning Each Small Move Into a Habit?

Simply put, habits = freedom.

Once a practice becomes a habit, it is automatic. We no longer have to devote time and energy toward its implementation. According to a study conducted by Duke University, as much as 45 percent of our behaviors are habitual (Guise, 2013). It seems prudent then to be conscientious about forming teacher habits that have positive effects on our students' learning. Just imagine if 45 percent of our actions in the classroom each day were both automatic and highly effective. Such a degree of automaticity would free up our brains. We would have the time and mental energy to focus on and think about more complicated concerns such as differentiating lessons for specific students or planning multiple resources for a given topic. We would have the space to think about and plan for the "big" things because our small habits require little to no thought. In essence, turning these simple, small moves into habits will give us instructional time back. Time we can devote to all the strategies, standards, expectations, and challenges that we currently do not have time for (Clear, 2018; Rubin, 2015). Having positive habits is particularly important during times of stress. When we are rested and calm, it is much easier to focus on developing new skills and improving our practice than when we are frazzled, overworked, and overwhelmed. When we become stressed (which is often) we fall back on our habits (even if they do not serve students well), so it makes sense to ensure that our habits are as beneficial to students as possible (Guise, 2013).

What Is a Keystone Habit?

According to Charles Duhigg (2014), who coined the phrase, a "keystone habit" is a habit that has the power to "start a chain reaction" (p. 100). He argues that not all habits are equal; some are more important than others in terms of creating a ripple effect of change within a person, a company, a community, or for our purposes, within a classroom. The idea is that focusing attention on one or more specific habits can potentially create enough change or disrupt current patterns enough to lead to the creation of other positive habits. Duhigg explains, "Keystone habits say that success doesn't depend on getting every single thing right, but instead relies on identifying a few key priorities and fashioning them into powerful levers" (pp. 100-101). This idea that we don't have to get everything right is very appealing to me. I didn't know it at the time, but I used the concept of keystone habits to help myself when I first began consulting with schools.

Prior to my first year of consulting, I exercised fairly regularly, ate a moderately healthy diet, and was upbeat and energetic the majority of the time. Over the course of my first year in this new role, however, I gained 15 pounds, virtually stopped exercising, and found myself battling bouts of frustration and anxiety. I kept telling myself it was just the newness of the job and that once I got settled in, I would get back to my routine. What I began to realize after months of this work that involved an ever-changing schedule and lots of travel was that there would be no "settling in." My new normal was always changing, day to day, week to week, and month to month.

I accepted that I wouldn't have a set routine, but I did not accept my added weight and change in mood, so on my one year anniversary of consulting, I made a promise to myself to eat right and take better care of myself. I was going to always make good food choices even on the road, go to bed early, and wake up every morning with enough time to exercise. Can you guess how long that plan lasted? Well, the following week I was scheduled to work in El Paso. I arrived at the airport after a full day of training at about 5:00 p.m. I was starving and rushing to make my flight, so I grabbed a not-so-healthy sandwich at the airport convenience store. As soon as I finished scarfing it down, the ticketing agent announced that our flight was delayed. I was supposed to land at 8:45 p.m. and would now be arriving at 11:00 p.m. Once in flight, we had to be diverted due to weather, so I did not get to my hotel until after midnight. My mood was sour, and I was hungry again so I gladly accepted the free chocolate chip cookies the hotel clerk offered. Internally I was thinking, "I deserve this splurge after what I've been through today." I set my alarm to exercise in the morning, but as I hit snooze, I convinced myself that I needed more sleep instead in order to be fresh for my training. My plan to eat right and take better care of myself had failed miserably.

Over the next several weeks, I failed at many more lofty and "all inclusive" attempts to make change in my life, so I decided to switch tactics. I decided to focus on a few specific changes and go from there. I also gave a lot of thought to these changes. They had to be things I could reasonably control even when traveling and even when complications occurred. Here was my list →

I picked these because they were "soft" enough to feel doable. I told myself that if I really needed a snack, I could still go buy one, just not from my hotel. Even though I had clothes and an alarm, it didn't mean I had to actually exercise. Over the next several weeks, these three changes did become habits, and I would argue they became my keystone habits. These three changes had the power to create a ripple effect within my life that resulted in many habits that I keep today to successfully manage my weight, my mood, and my unpredictable schedule. Let's take a closer look:

When I committed to packing exercise clothes every time I traveled, I no longer negotiated with myself while packing about whether I'd want to exercise or would have time to exercise. I just packed the clothes. Knowing I had them with me, I started making a point to look at the exercise room at the hotel when I checked in. This got me thinking about exactly what my workout might entail the next morning. When I'd get to my room, as I would hang up my professional clothes for the next day, I'd see the workout clothes. I started laying them out as well, thinking, "If I take these out, then I won't need as much time in the morning. It'll all be ready." When my alarm would go off and I'd hit snooze, I'd think about those clothes already being ready,

1. Always pack exercise clothes when traveling

2. Always have an alarm set to go off early enough to be able to work out

3. No more getting snacks from the hotel

making it more difficult for me to fall back asleep. All of these little steps laid the groundwork for me to actually get up. After several times of not having a specific plan for what I was going to do when I got to the hotel exercise room, I began using my flight time to jot down a workout on a post-it note. I'd put that by my bedside table. While none of these decisions/actions resulted in 100 percent success at exercising, I moved from making excuses to actually working out most days that I traveled.

Not eating snacks from the hotel worked the same way. Even if I craved the cookies upon check-in, I rarely had enough energy to leave my hotel to go get a snack at a nearby store, so I'd just not have a snack. The no snacking habit spread into my training days. Most places where I train provide chocolates or other candies on the tables for participants, and I started telling myself, "Ok, Nancy, no mini candy bar until at least the afternoon." This turned into no chocolates at all, which turned into me buying sugar-free mints that I kept in my work bag. After not eating unhealthy snacks for a while, I felt more confident in my choice to eat right, and I began making better lunch and dinner choices. After all, I didn't want to ruin the progress I had made by eliminating cookies and chocolate with a giant cheeseburger at lunch. Once I was in the habit of eating fairly well, I made a big goal: save all of my "bad" eating for the weekends when I am with my family. My small keystone habit of no snacks at the hotel rippled over time into additional changes to my diet that resulted in success with my big change of "eating clean" when I am traveling.

Ten years later, I have long since lost the extra weight, am back to my energetic self

and most importantly have habits in place that maximize my ability to meet my personal goals of eating right and taking better care of myself. So much so that many of my clients poke fun at me when I arrive for a training, saying, "What would you like to eat for lunch? Let me guess, grilled chicken salad, no cheese, no croutons, dressing on the side, right?" Their comments only reinforce my good habits. I reply, "You got it."

Keystone habits are just as powerful within our classrooms. The idea is to pick a few small changes (or maybe even just one to start) that have the potential to shift our teaching patterns in a different direction. Instead of thinking "all or nothing," think, "What is one adjustment I can make that can lead to more positive change?" Each of the 23 small moves in this book could become a keystone habit. For example, if you want your students to "think more," rather than completely changing your lesson design, focus on one small move in chapter 2 that feels doable, like giving your students a clear purpose for reading (see p. 51). Once setting a purpose for reading becomes a habit, it will begin to inform many other aspects of your instruction. You'll become more explicit in setting purposes for other tasks; you'll begin to look for other ways to support critical thinking. Over time, the ripple effect of one keystone habit will allow you to meet your goal: to have students think more.

Let's take a look at how the idea of keystone habits played out in my classroom. After several years of teaching, I was feeling pretty confident in my abilities. I had strong classroom management, well-designed lessons, and an engaging teaching style. I was teaching English Language Arts and Reading at the time and had an incredible team of fellow ELAR teachers that year. We met weekly to plan together and often looked at data to inform our instruction. I was seen as a leader within the group and usually created the agendas and ran the meetings. My students' scores were generally average to high compared to the other classes, but they were never as high as Ms. Mayo's kids. I knew most of her students, and she did not have a class full of overachievers or gifted students; they had the same challenges as (if not more than) my own kids. Week after week I'd wonder how it was possible that her students were outperforming mine on common assessments and assignments. Because I am super competitive, I finally asked. She said she didn't know because she just follows the weekly plan that we all set out. Now, Ms. Mayo was not being evasive; she is a genuinely sweet, hardworking, and quiet person. I knew she had to be doing something different, however, and I needed to know what it was. Since she couldn't articulate it to me, and I couldn't go watch her teach, I decided in that moment that I would "study" her during our meetings.

Enter small move #1: Listen to everything that Ms. Mayo says. I remained an active participant in our meetings, but whenever Ms. Mayo spoke, I'd stop and listen. Not listen so that I could add on to her idea or share something I was doing, but just really listen. I found after several weeks of doing this that her comments were almost always specific to a single item on an assignment or test. Instead of saying, "Yeah, my kids struggled with the main idea on this one" (the type of comment I would make). She'd say, "Guys, look at number 11 on Thursday's passage. Most of my kids picked C instead of B. I think they got thrown off because it was a main idea, just of a paragraph not the

entire passage." Her comments were directly related to how her students performed on the daily work from that week. She used data from graded assignments to make real-time adjustments to her teaching. For example, the day after noticing the confusion with number 11, she'd spend a couple of minutes reteaching or clarifying that question with her students. You might be thinking that this seems like a normal and obvious practice, but it presented a major roadblock for me. You see, I hate grading papers. While I'd never admit it in those meetings, I had not graded most of the assignments my peers were discussing in the weekly meetings. I had many great teaching habits, and I also had this one terrible habit: I did almost all of my grading beginning two days before progress reports were due. I didn't have a clear picture of what my students were actually learning from any given lesson until two or three weeks after I taught it. I knew I needed to fix this.

Much like my previous weight loss example, I started with a lofty goal of grading every assignment before I left campus on the day my students turned it in. That worked for a day or two, but then staff meetings, a last-minute invite for dinner, or a vet appointment would get in the way. On top of that, I still dreaded the thought of grading an entire class's assignment. I knew I needed to make this more manageable, so I made two small changes:

1. **I moved the "turn-in" tray from a shelf on the side of my room to the center of my desk.**

2. **Instead of grading everything every day, I decided that I only had to grade three students' papers before I left: Alex's, Serena's, and Michael's.**

I did not define these two changes as "key-stone" habits at the time, but they absolutely became the small moves that started a chain reaction. I made the first change, moving the tray, for the sole purpose of irritation. The papers to be graded were now physically in front of me everyday. I keep a really clean desk, and my students do not keep a really clean tray. Whenever I'd go to my desk to grab a sip of water, give a student the stapler, or check email (during my planning period, of course), I'd see this messy pile of papers. It irritated me every time. This created a disruption in my brain that never went away until I fixed it. Multiple times a day, I'd straighten the papers up, and it was impossible to leave without making my desk tidy. This doesn't mean I would grade the papers, but I always saw them and organized them.

successful. It only took me a few minutes to grade three papers, and I always had a targeted reteaching or clarification for the following day based on those papers.

After a few weeks of building the three-paper grading habit, I found that it rippled into more. Once I sat down to grade those three, I often ended up wondering how other specific students did, so I'd find their papers and grade them. Over time, sitting down at the end of the day to grade "a little" turned into me planning to grade for 30 minutes as soon as I finished car pick-up or bus duty. I became more efficient in my grading processes. More importantly, I paid attention to each student's errors. I found myself keeping short notes about the errors on a post-it note, and then I'd use that post-it note to adjust my warm-up for

I did not define these two changes as "keystone" habits at the time, but they absolutely became the small moves that started a chain reaction.

The second change, grading three specific students' papers each day, was also transformative. Alex, Serena, and Michael were three students who fell into the "bubble" category. They were always on the bubble of success or failure on any given assignment. I selected them because I thought the way these three students performed on any given assignment would give me an accurate reflection of any challenges or misunderstandings my class as a whole might be having. I could use what I learned from their successes and mistakes to inform my teaching the following day (and I wouldn't have to commit to grading everyone's paper). I viewed Alex's, Serena's, and Michael's papers as my formative assessment shortcut. This plan was immediately

the following day, ensuring that I addressed some of the errors from the day before.

Without realizing it, I was in fact grading almost all of my students' work on the day they completed it. My teaching became so informed by what they produced that I started to almost crave seeing their work. Even when handing an assignment out in class, I'd already be thinking, "I wonder how many are going to get confused by number seven," or "I really hope Alex remembers what we reviewed in today's warm-up when he starts this."

As you can imagine, my students began making accelerated growth, and their scores on common assessments reflected that. In one semester I changed from a teacher who "coasted" on some natural talent, which resulted in students making average gains, to a teacher who made frequent and intentional adjustments based on data, which resulted in students making significant gains. We all know formative assessment should inform our teaching, but the only way I was able to put that into practice was thanks to a messy turn-in tray and three students' papers. These were the two keystone habits that created enough disruption to my current situation to make way for the formation of a new and effective teaching practice.

How Do I Turn Small Moves Into Habits?

This is the most important question in the book. None of the small moves are complicated or time consuming, so on the surface it appears easy to implement all of them. The problem is remembering to make the move when it is needed. Remembering is hard. We often have 17 different thoughts going through our minds while we are teaching ("I've got to explain this a different way... Daniel needs to quit being so disruptive in the chat...Where did I link that video?...Did this class finish yesterday's assignment?...The bell is about to ring and I need to show them their homework...What do you need, Aracely?...Yes ok, so as I was saying..."). Instead of needing to remember to execute each move, what if we made them automatic? What if each move was a habit? What if making each move was so ingrained that it happened without any thought at all? Well, that would be awesome! So how do we make the ideas in this book habits? Again, we can rely on the work of experts in the field of habit formation. There is a wide variety of suggestions and techniques for how to build habits, but one recommendation remains constant across

all of them: accountability (DuHigg, 2014; Rubin, 2015; Lemov et al., 2012; Clear, 2018; Davenport, 2016). When we are trying to turn a small move into a habit, we need to be held accountable for our actions. Feeling accountable can be motivated by a wide variety of emotions (integrity, fear of embarrassment, pride, etc.) and can also stem from a variety of sources (peers, students, boss, self, etc.). We see the effect of accountability throughout our daily lives. The person who works out with a paid trainer will generally work out harder than the person exercising alone. When students know that their stories are going to be part of a Parent Night slideshow, they usually put more effort into their details and illustrations than they might for an everyday journal entry. If you and a colleague are both interviewing for the same position, you will likely prepare more diligently for the interview than if you knew you were the only applicant.

As a teacher, you see and feel the effect of accountability as well. Certainly our students' performance on state-mandated assessments is an obvious form of accountability, but it is critical to think through and build accountability systems that are more localized and more frequently occurring than a single end-of-year test. Often teachers are "islands unto themselves." Unlike many other professions where people work alongside others and are interdependent, teachers often work in isolation with their students day in and day out. Because we work solo most of the time, we need to create ways to hold ourselves accountable. I think we all strive to take ownership over our instruction and accept responsibility for the learning opportunities we provide to our students, but it can be very challenging to sustain high levels of personal accountability without some outside support.

- **Tell your class what you are doing and ask for their help.** For example, if you want to focus on turning the *Listen For …* small move (see p. 54) into a habit, you might tell your class, "Whenever we look at video clips, I want to give you a purpose for listening, so when I pull up YouTube or am about to start a BrainPop video, can you please remind me to give you a purpose?" Most students might not remember to do so, but there is always that one super conscientious kid who will!

- **Enlist the help of a colleague.** Together with another teacher, select a small move and practice it. Set predetermined times to check in with each other about how it's going. Let's pretend you and another biology teacher want to help your students, especially your English learners, speak in complete sentences. You two decide to focus on implementing the *Package and Parrot* small move (see p. 24). Checking in with your fellow teacher could be as simple and frequent as making eye contact across the hall during each passing period and showing with your hands the number of times you remembered to use *Package and Parrot* that period. Even if you forgot to do it during first period, seeing your fellow teacher's gestured number will hold you accountable for refocusing on it during second period. Interestingly, with the rise of virtual learning, many teams of teachers are experiencing an increase in collaboration via a virtual "meet up." Planning a mutually agreeable (and brief) time to talk in a remote setting might actually be a better way for both of you to focus on supporting each other.

- **Announce your goal to your administration and support staff.** Doug Lemov (2012) refers to this as "calling your shot," or informing anyone who will be observing you about the techniques you are focused on (p. 86). Select a small move, and let anyone who enters your virtual or face-to-face classroom know that you'd like for them to look for that move. Knowing others are looking for it increases your awareness.

- **Keep a record of implementation of the small move.** This might be a simple tally on your dry erase board; you might write a short reflection at the end of the day, create some sort of easy charting system, or use an online resource for tracking.

- **Capitalize on the power of social media.** You can post about your small moves and enlist the support of innumerable online peers.

In addition to finding ways to increase accountability, there are many other strategies for habit formation. Below you'll find summaries of additional ideas from scientists, psychologists, authors, and other experts for how to turn a small move into a habit.

DESCRIPTION/SOURCE	REAL LIFE EXAMPLE	CLASSROOM EXAMPLE
Repetition Repeat the small move over and over again. Each repetition will make the move easier for next time. Making choices is exhausting to our brain, and repetition leads to automation. Source: Guise, 2013, *Mini Habits: Smaller Habits, Bigger Results*	Both of my parents' cars had manual transmissions, so I had to learn to drive using a stick shift. At the beginning, I would stall out the majority of the time. After lots of repetition (and laughter), however, I began to figure out the right combination of releasing the clutch and giving gas. With continued practice, driving a car with a manual transmission became automatic to me.	You want students to elaborate and explain their answer choices when reviewing multiple choice assignments. When students give their answer choices, follow up by prompting them with "because …" After every student response, repeat your prompt, "because …" Over time students will naturally state their answer choices and follow them with "because …" For more details, see *Prove It* on p. 30.
Two Minute Rule Scale down any habit/goal/change you desire into the smallest and easiest version. Your first efforts should take two minutes or less. The idea is to "show up," or to start. If beginning feels overwhelming, no action takes place. With a "two minute or less" start, you are offering yourself a "gateway habit" that will lead to the full realization of your goal later on. Source: Clear, 2018, *Atomic Habits: An Easy and Proven Way to Build Good Habits & Break Bad Ones*	You want to run a 5K, but you currently do not run at all. The two minute "gateway habit" could be simply putting on your running shoes. Doing only that "opens the door" for you to take the next step.	You want to manage your instructional time better because you always feel like tasks take too long. The two minute "gateway habit" could be to open a timer app on your phone. For more details, see *Timer* on p. 78.
Monitoring Select a habit and track/record every time you do it. Often we overestimate or underestimate our actions. Having an accurate count makes it impossible to ignore reality and often positively affects future choices. Source: Rubin, 2015, *Better Than Before*	The most common example of monitoring is keeping a food journal. Many apps and devices also track the number of steps you take in a given day.	If you want to increase student conversations during instruction, keep a tally on your board for every time you give kids an opportunity to talk to each other. Another option is to record yourself teaching and, while watching it, write down the number of times you made any given small move.

DESCRIPTION/SOURCE	REAL LIFE EXAMPLE	CLASSROOM EXAMPLE
Habit Stacking Connect a new habit you'd like to create with an existing habit. This concept can be expanded into a series of habits that then become a routine. Source: Scott, 2014, *Habit Stacking* and others	I've worn contact lenses since the fourth grade. I put them in every morning and take them out every night. A couple of years ago when I began needing to take a daily medication, I had trouble remembering to take it. My solution was to literally (and figuratively) stack my medicine on top of my lens case. Now every night I take out my lenses and put my medication bottle on top of the case. In the morning, I take my medicine and then put in my contacts.	We all turn on or power up our computers each morning. Connect that habit with writing your objectives in a color-coded way. As soon as you turn the computer on, walk to where you display objectives and begin color-coding them while your computer boots up. If your objectives are displayed online, you can habit stack color coding your objectives with entering your login information or updating your virtual classroom's main page. For more details, see *Color-Code* on p. 71.
Visual Cues Connect an object, picture, or person with the habit you'd like to create. Use that visual to cue you or remind you to execute the habit.	Every morning I take my dogs outside, and while I know they need to be fed as well, I often get distracted by my daughters or my phone. To remedy this, I have put my dogs' food bowls right next to the back door (which I pass every morning to let them out). I also keep the dog food right in front of where I keep coffee filters (I never forget to make coffee). The combination of those visual cues (seeing the bowls and seeing the food) reminds me to feed them.	Select one to two students in each class who are especially jolly. Mentally make them your visual cue to remember to smile. Every time you make eye contact with them on your virtual platform, or look in their direction it will remind you to smile. Note: This is particularly important if you have a challenging class or are teaching virtually. For more details, see *Smile* on p. 66.

Executing some form of accountability system along with any combination of the techniques listed above will transform any small move into a habit that you can rely on. Once you build one great habit, move on to another. Building the first habit might require more extended time and effort, but with each new habit you form, the habits themselves become easier. Engaging in the ongoing practice of building habits will, over time, make you more efficient at habit formation itself.

02

Teacher Habits That *Help Kids* to *Talk More*

The focus of this chapter is talk. Specifically, it is filled with small moves that will help you get students to speak more frequently and more effectively in an academic setting.

These moves will help you increase both the quantity and quality of classroom conversations. Speaking effectively in an academic setting is more critical than ever before as our world is becoming more interconnected. Spend time reading any educational journal, and you will be inundated with articles and research about the power of student conversation in the classroom.

One study from Music Educators Journal (2011) found that "classrooms with an interactive participant structure, in which students are given the opportunity to share and develop knowledge with their peers, can lead to a much more meaningful learning environment" (p. 51). Similar benefits can be found in a science classroom. In their article, "Entering the Conversation: Exploratory Talk in Middle School Science," Cervetti et al. (2014) explain that "science discourse can support students' development of conceptual understandings and reasoning, participation in inquiry, and ability to explain and communicate science understand-ings" (p. 548). In her book *Conversations,* Regie Routman (2000) states, "All learning involves conversation. The ongoing dialogue, internal and external, that occurs as we read, write, listen, compose, observe, refine, interpret, and analyze is how we learn" (p. xxxvi).

If the current research supports student talk, why aren't more teachers planning opportuni-ties for it? The short answer is that when we let students talk, often times, bad stuff happens.

In other words, there are frequently different roadblocks that get in the way of students expe-riencing success during conversation.

I spend time in hundreds of classrooms per year. I've observed a wide variety of techniques and strategies for student talk. After a decade of observations, this is the biggest generalization I can make about student talk: conversation is relatively commonplace, but highly effective academic conversation is not. My goal with the seven small moves in this chapter is to fix that one tiny step at a time. This chapter offers ideas to build habits for facilitating student talk that ensures equitable sharing among all students, an increase in academic language use, and most importantly, scaffolds for students who may lack confidence, language proficiency, or even interest.

SMALL MOVE	TARGET
• **Package and Parrot** • **Target the Talk** • **Prove It (a.k.a. Because ...)**	Increase academic language use
• **Appointed Roles**	Ensure equitable participation among all students
• **Anyone's Idea** • **Prep the Speaker** • **Plus Minus**	Support students who feel discomfort or stress related to talking tasks

Package and Parrot

Package and Parrot is a small move for responding to students when they give an accurate but partial answer. The teacher "packages" the student response in a complete sentence and then asks the class to "parrot" (or repeat) that response. Younger learners enjoy and benefit from abundant use of this move. In contrast, it is better to use it sparingly with older students; for example, use it specifically when working with challenging vocabulary, or to reach an essential understanding.

Challenge a Bad Habit

Often the teacher is the only person in the classroom who is actually using the academic vocabulary of the lesson. Even when students understand the content, they may not be acquiring the academic language because they aren't expected to use it. Consider this interaction:

TEACHER: Which operation do you think we should use to solve this problem?

SIMONE: We need to do times.

TEACHER: Do you mean multiplication? (*Simone nods to indicate yes.*) Why do you think multiplication?

SIMONE: It's four girls, and they all have nine bracelets.

TEACHER: Ok good. So the girls are our groups, and each group has nine bracelets. Everyone go ahead and make your model on your paper.

While Simone had accurate information, there is a huge discrepancy between her word choice and her teacher's. Her teacher used the language of the lesson (operation, solve, problem, multiplication, groups, each, model), but Simone did not.

Implement a Better Habit:
Package and Parrot

Package: When a student offers information that is limited to just a word, term, or phrase, restate their response in a complete thought. Think of the student response as a gift that we are just wrapping up for them, making it pretty, if you will.

Parrot: Ask the class to repeat the complete thought you just packaged. Consider that in doing so, all students receive the "gift" of the answer in a complete form. They are now using the academic language rather than just hearing it.

Note: This small move is useful when creating the expectation that students share their ideas in complete thoughts using the language of the lesson. It is more efficient for you to "package and parrot" rather than perhaps embarrassing a student by saying, "You're right, but can you say that in a complete sentence?" Over time students will consistently meet your expectations about how to share their thinking, making this move necessary only in isolated situations.

Why Is This Small Move Significant?

We all want students to be able to communicate their learning accurately and completely. This quick move builds what I call "linguistic momentum." It gives kids a low stress way to start using terms and formal speech structures. Each time students "parrot" our model, we are normalizing the use of academic language.

CLASSROOM EXAMPLE - ELEMENTARY

TEACHER: Which operation do you think we should use to solve this problem?

SIMONE: We need to do times.

TEACHER: Do you mean multiplication? *(Simone nods to indicate yes.)* I agree, we should use multiplication to solve this problem. Let's all repeat that.

TEACHER WITH CLASS: We should use multiplication to solve this problem.

TEACHER: Now, Simone, why do you think we should use multiplication to solve this problem?

SIMONE: It's four girls, and they all have nine bracelets.

TEACHER: Ok good. So the girls are our groups. Everyone, tell your partner, "We have four groups." *(Students turn to partners and repeat, "We have four groups.")* And Simone is right, we have nine bracelets in each group. Everyone, whisper that to your pinkie. *(Students whisper to their pinkies, "We have nine bracelets in each group.")*

CLASSROOM EXAMPLE - SECONDARY (CHEMISTRY)

**Given the image below is displayed on the board during a Chemistry class

TEACHER: Ok everyone, let's look at this isotope notation and review what we've learned. What can you tell me about Boron?

MARIAH: There are five protons.

TEACHER: Yes! How do you know?

MARIAH: That is the number on the bottom left, the atomic number, right?

TEACHER:Yes! *(Pointing to the number 5)* The atomic number tells the number of protons. Everybody, say that with me real quickly: "The atomic number tells the number of protons." *(Class begrudgingly repeats.)*

TEACHER: Now what about the number 9 above it?

JASON: *(shouts out)* Nine neutrons!

TEACHER: No, it is not nine neutrons. This 9 is the mass number, which is made up of two things.

DARNELL and several others: *(shouts out)* Neutrons and protons!

TEACHER: Yes! Everyone, look up here. This is a mistake that I see a lot so I want to make sure we all have it clear. This 9 does not represent just neutrons. It is the number of neutrons and protons put together. *(Touching the 9)* The mass number is protons PLUS neutrons. Everybody say that. *(Half the class mumbles it.)* Y'all, for real, most people get questions wrong because of this. Everybody say this with me: "The mass number is protons PLUS neutrons." *(The class repeats.)*

VARIATIONS

- When the academic vocabulary is visible on your students' device or is posted somewhere in the room, track it with your cursor or point to it as you ask. This cues your student in a nonverbal way to use those specific words.

- Give students an interesting direction for where to parrot. For example,
  "Say it to your knee."
  "Say it to your partner's shoulder."
  "Say it to the flag."

- Give students a fun or unexpected way to parrot. For example,
  "Say it like a pirate."
  "Say it like you are really bored."
  "Say it like you are freezing cold."

- When using this technique in a virtual setting, it is important to consider if you want students to stay muted or unmute when they parrot. Asking them to stay muted allows all virtual learners to hear only your high quality model; whereas asking students to unmute often increases compliance.

Target the Talk

This small move occurs immediately before student-to-student conversation. The teacher tells students exactly what academic vocabulary she wants them to use during their discussion.

Challenge a Bad Habit

At the end of my first year of teaching, my principal asked what my plans were for the summer. After outlining my still-fuzzy summer agenda, she volun-told me to include getting ESL certified in those plans. She explained that it would be great for my career, that I'd earn a $500 stipend ($84.32 after taxes, right?), and most importantly, that she really needed me to help our English learners next year. Always up for a challenge, I agreed. Despite having had very little professional development regarding English learners, I was a good test taker and earned my certification. Upon returning to school for my second year, I had a class roster that included a majority of English learners.

While I was, admittedly, ill-equipped to meet my students' linguistic needs, I did know a few things, one of which was that they needed to talk. My English learners would not acquire more English unless they had a chance to use it. Knowing this, I did "think pair shares" and "turn and talks" all the time. Multiple times in each lesson, my students were able to talk with a partner or their table mates about what they were learning. They became less shy, and I felt confident that they were all acquiring more English.

That second year of teaching was hard work, with many ups and downs, but as my students and I entered "testing season," we were all feeling good. However, the feeling only lasted until I received my students' TELPAS (Texas English Language Proficiency Assessment System) results back. Less than 50 percent of my English learners had increased at least one level in their language proficiency. I was devastated and felt like I had failed them. I was speechless when I saw that even in the speaking domain, only a handful of my hard-working students had demonstrated growth. How could this be? They talked all the time!

I wish I could go back to my second-year-teacher self and tell her, "Talk isn't enough!" The opportunity to speak (which was plentiful in my room) is not equivalent to a structured plan for students to use the language of the lesson. You see, even though my students were talking a lot, they were only using the English words with which they were comfortable.

Let's look at an example. Imagine my class was solving a two-digit by two-digit addition problem (15 + 44) for their math warm-up, which is a review of the previous day's learning. In this scenario, I asked my students to turn to their partners and explain how they solved the problem. Here is what typically happened:

> ALICIA (*to Michael, her partner*): Umm ... I did 5 and 4 and got 9 and then did this one (*pointing to the tens place*) for 5, so I got 59.

> MICHAEL (*to Alicia*): Me too. 59.

Did Michael and Alicia do what I asked them to do? Yes ... with the words in English that they were comfortable with and already "owned." Did they acquire more academic English as a result of this opportunity to talk? I do not believe so.

In order for our English learners Michael and Alicia (and any other students) to acquire academic English, we have to ensure they are actually using the words and phrases about which they are learning. This is easier to accomplish than you might think. All we have to do is ask them to use them. Simply put, we tell them the words we want to hear right before we ask them to speak. I call this "Target the Talk."

Implement a Better Habit: *Target the Talk*

1. Identify words or phrases you would like students to use during a particular conversation.

2. Immediately before you give students an opportunity to talk to each other, tell them what you would like to hear. My "go-to" phrases for targeting student talk:

> *I'm listening for ...*
> *Use these words ...*
> *Here's your stem ...*
> *It should sound like ...*

Why Is This Small Move Significant?

Can you imagine how much language our students will acquire if every time we ask them to speak to each other, we use one of these phrases? When we consistently target student conversation, they not only use the new vocabulary, but they become more comfortable with speaking in a more formal and academic way. We are thus normalizing academic conversation.

CLASSROOM EXAMPLE

Let's go back to the previous example. What are the academic words or phrases I would want to hear? How about "ones place," "tens place," "sum," and "equals." I might want to focus on phrases like "number sentence" or "solved the problem." So how do I "target their talk" toward these terms? I simply ask the students to use them. Here are some options for how that might sound:

> *Please explain how you solved the problem to your partner. I'm listening for you to use the words "ones place" and "tens place."*
>
> *When it is your turn, use this stem: "I solved this addition number sentence by ..."*
>
> *As you talk with your partner, use the words from our anchor chart. Let's read them together: "addition," "equals," "sum."*

If I had used any of the phrases above, the overwhelming majority of my class would have followed those directions, which would have resulted in each of them actually using the academic English of the lesson.

Variations

• As students acclimate to using academic vocabulary with each other, I am less specific about telling them the words. Rather I direct them to a resource, which may sound like this: "Remember to use your words from the _____ (word wall, anchor chart, smart board, slide deck)," or "Open your _____ (journals, notes), and use them while you talk."

• Post the phrases for targeting the talk on your walls to serve as a visual reminder for you to do it.

• Use this same small move when students are communicating virtually. For example, also target the words/phrases just before you ask them to reply using the chat, discuss in a breakout room, or record themselves using apps like Flipgrid or Seesaw.

Prove It (a.k.a. Because ...)

In this small move, the teacher moves beyond seeking the correct answer but also ensures that students prove how they know they are correct. Asking students to use the word "because" in their responses is an easy way to build this habit.

Challenge a Bad Habit

At times I am guilty of what I call "machine gun" questioning. This is the rapid fire Q&A that consists of a multitude of basic questions followed by a quick succession of short student responses. While this type of questioning might have a place for rote review of procedures, it often bleeds into other parts of my lessons, where it has a detrimental effect. When I ask questions to check for understanding in a "machine gun" style, it is easy to think that my students' understanding of any given concept is more developed than it actually is. Every time we push through to the next topic or question instead of prompting students to explain their idea, we are both limiting their practice at critically thinking and operating from a false sense of what they know. Just because they can give me brief and correct answers doesn't mean that they can articulate why their answers are correct or how they generated their answers. Consistently prompting students to prove their reasoning gives them the practice they need to explain their ideas more completely.

Implement a Better Habit: *Prove It*

1. Before calling on students to answer a question, remind them that you are listening for the word "because."

2. If students reply without explaining their ideas fully, ask them to "prove it." Here are some sample prompts you might use:

Tell me more about that.

What makes you say that?

How did you come up with your answer?

What evidence do you have for that answer?

Why Is This Small Move Significant?

Asking students to "prove it" is significant because it requires them to extend their thinking beyond just their initial responses. When this becomes a regular practice, it promotes a mindset geared toward explanation and evidence rather than just a correct answer (Ritchhart et al., 2011). Another key aspect to asking students to "prove it" is that you gain a better understanding of where they are in their learning of the content. Their extended responses let you know whether or not they are on track, and you know exactly where you can provide feedback to help them. You do not get that sort of information from a one-word answer.

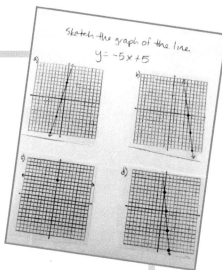

Sketch the graph of the line.
$y = -5x + 5$

CLASSROOM EXAMPLE

Mrs. Dismukes just asked her Algebra I class
which answer choice best represents $y = -5x+5$.

Non-Example

MRS. DISMUKES: Allison, which line
did you select?

ALLISON: D

MRS. DISMUKES: Awesome! That is correct. Everyone else, double
check that you picked answer choice D.

Example

MRS. DISMUKES: Allison, which line did you select?

ALLISON: D.

MRS. DISMUKES: How do you know that is correct?

ALLISON: Something was wrong with all the others. Like in A, the
slope is five instead of negative five.

MRS. DISMUKES: You're right. What about answer choices B and C?

ALLISON: In B the slope is right, but they started the graph on the
x-axis not the y-axis. And C, that is just $y = 5$.

MRS. DISMUKES: Good job. Does anyone have any
questions about why D is correct?

Variations

- Ask students to "prove it" in writing by annotating a question that is in multiple choice format. See example to the right.

- In a virtual setting, utilize the chat feature or a student-specific shared slide so everyone has a chance to "prove it" in writing even if they aren't called on.

- When students are reading independently, encourage them to annotate anything they mark or highlight.

- For students at the very beginning levels of English proficiency, proof can also be a gesture. (E.g., Touch the line on the text that helped you identify the author's purpose.)

- Create a *Prove It* **anchor chart** to display in the classroom that has specific sentence stems for students to use.
  It might look like this ⟶

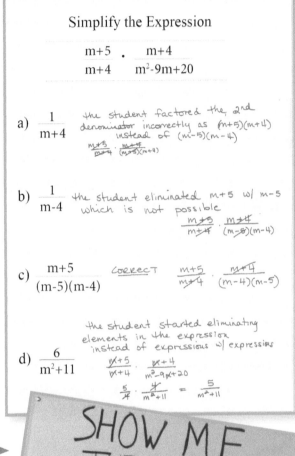

Simplify the Expression

$$\frac{m+5}{m+4} \cdot \frac{m+4}{m^2-9m+20}$$

a) $\dfrac{1}{m+4}$ the student factored the 2nd denominator incorrectly as (m+5)(m+4) instead of (m-5)(m-4)

b) $\dfrac{1}{m-4}$ the student eliminated m+5 w/ m-5 which is not possible

c) $\dfrac{m+5}{(m-5)(m-4)}$ CORRECT

d) $\dfrac{6}{m^2+11}$ the student started eliminating elements in the expression instead of expressions w/ expressions

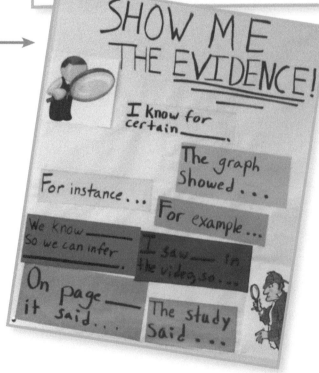

SHOW ME THE EVIDENCE!

I know for certain _____.

The graph showed . . .

For instance . . .

For example . . .

We know _____
So we can infer _____.

I saw _____ in the video, so . . .

On page _____ it said . . .

The study said . . .

Appointed Roles

In this small move, the teacher gives each person a title or role which allows her to ensure more equitable participation. Labeling each person's role minimizes the ability for some students to "fly under the radar."

Challenge a Bad Habit

What I mean by appointing roles is giving students a specific "job" during a conversation, which in turn gives the teacher a system for managing how they participate in class. When we ask partners to "turn and talk," normally the most extroverted student begins and the more introverted student listens. Often the more confident student shares while the less confident student watches and usually the most knowledgeable students answer first while the less knowledgeable students simply agree with them. We see this with adults too. If you are Zooming with your team at a virtual faculty meeting and your principal asks a question, I bet you know exactly who will do the talking for your team. We've all been to trainings where one or two participants dominate the day with their stories, comments, and questions. This move is about minimizing the ability for some students to "take over" and maximizing equitable participation.

Implement a Better Habit: *Appointed Roles*

1. Think of how students collaborate in your class, and give them specific labels that correspond. For example:

   - Kindergarteners, sitting on colored squares on the carpet, can be assigned blue/yellow partners and red/green partners.
   - Students who are seated at desks in rows can be assigned A/B partners.
   - If students are collaborating virtually in groups of 4, they can number off.

2. When you ask students to collaborate, use those assigned roles to tell students who will speak first. For example:

   Blue and red partners go first; yellow and green partners go second.

   B's talk first, and A's, you talk second.

   In your breakout room, number 3s share first, then 2s, then 1s, and finally 4s.

3. The next time students collaborate, alternate who speaks first using the same labels. For example:

   This time yellow and green partners go first, and then blue and red.

   A's you're up first; B's you'll be next.

   Number 1s share first and then go in numerical order.

Why Is This Small Move Significant?

When we regularly alternate who will participate first, our students learn several valuable lessons. Namely, everyone's ideas are valued and everyone's voice matters. Students who may feel discomfort when participating begin to gain confidence because they now have what Schultz (2012) calls a "predictable partner" (p. 25). All students experience an increase in accountability. That is, students who might previously have been "coasting" through collaborative tasks by being passive are now participating. There is also value for the students who tend to do all the talking. They now have the opportunity to hear new ideas from their peers and often learn from them.

Variations

• Have fun with the labels. Instead of A/B partners, use milk and cookies or Texans and Astros, etc.

• Use content vocabulary for the labels. Instead of A/B, use potential and kinetic or numerators and denominators, etc.

• Use personal characteristics for the labels, like shortest hair shares first, or the person with the most letters in their first name speaks first.

• Assign each student an "away partner" (another student who does NOT sit near them). This creative pairing is an efficient way for students to move around the classroom and find their partner wihtout wasting time.

• Once students become accustomed to participating equally, you can often just say, "Make sure you are switching who shares first."

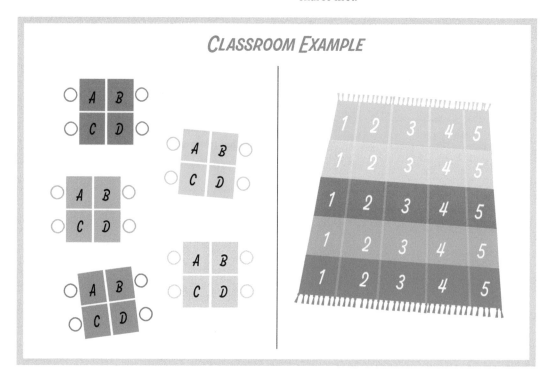

CLASSROOM EXAMPLE

SMALL MOVE 2.5
Anyone's Idea

In this small move, the teacher encourages the student who has been called upon to share either his own idea or an idea he heard from his partner, group, table, etc. This move is focused on helping students feel comfortable participating in class.

Challenge a Bad Habit

Imagine this scenario: You are teaching a synchronous math class via Zoom. You ask students to talk about how to solve a problem in breakout rooms. You join each breakout to monitor while they collaborate, and you hear some really great thinking in each group. As you close the breakouts and bring everyone back to the main room, you are feeling confident that they are with you. You want to generate some whole-group sharing, so you plan to call on a few students to share what their groups discussed. You call on your first student, and she freezes. You ask the question again and encourage her with a gentle, "You know this." Your student remains silent.

We have all taught students who feel uncomfortable speaking in front of the whole class. Some freeze up, others shrug their shoulders, and some even physically shrink a little. Their discomfort can be so palatable that it is easy to move the attention off of them and onto a more willing student. *Anyone's Idea* offers us another possibility: creating a more comfortable way for the original student to answer.

Implement a Better Habit: *Anyone's Idea*

1. Ask a question.
2. Give students an opportunity to discuss the answer with a partner or group.
3. Use a random selection technique to call on a student.
4. Give the selected student some options for what to share. It could sound like this:

   - *Feel free to share your idea or any ideas that your group discussed.*

   - *You can tell your answer or your partner's answer.*

   - *Can you give us one of the comments that came out of your discussion? It doesn't have to be yours.*

   - *Please share the answer you thought was the best.*

Why Is This Small Move Significant?

Giving students options for what information they share lowers the pressure they may feel. It can eliminate the fear of "What if I am wrong?" It also allows the speaker to have more control over the answer itself. The student can share what she thinks was the best response even if it did not originate from her. Teachers do not necessarily need to make this move for all students. Our most extroverted and confident students are usually happy to answer in class. For students who feel anxious when they are asked to answer a question, however, it can dramatically increase their willingness to participate and improve the content of their answers. This move helps students feel more like "reporters" of information rather than feeling like they need to be the "experts" about the information.

Variations

· Periodically require that students share someone else's idea rather than just offering it as an option. This increases accountability for the listeners during collaboration.

· When you call on a student, encourage his partner to stand with the selected student so he does not feel alone. This is particularly supportive in primary grades.

CLASSROOM EXAMPLE

Mr. Ortiz's English class has just finished reading *The Great Gatsby* by F. Scott Fitzgerald. Today's objective centers around how the author uses different colors within the story to symbolize various themes. Small groups of students are given a few excerpts that are linked by a common color. Their task is to discuss how that particular color is symbolic of one of the themes in the novel. After several minutes of discussion, Mr. Ortiz calls on a student from the first group. His name is Terrell. Mr. Ortiz notices from Terrell's body language that he is uncomfortable.

MR. ORTIZ: Terrell, what color did your group have?

TERRELL: Green.

MR. ORTIZ: Ok great. So how does the color green symbolize one of our themes? You can share anyone's idea from your group discussion.

Prep the Speaker

After partners or small groups of students collaborate, the teacher gives a short amount of time for the group to prepare their speaker. During this time, groups determine their best answer and the speaker can practice what he is going to say before he shares it with the entire class.

Challenge a Bad Habit

My students had many opportunities to collaborate with each other throughout class. After each of these small-group conversations, I would select a speaker from each group to share out with the whole class. Once I picked each speaker, however, guess what the other group members usually did? Either they would point and laugh at the speaker ("Haha! Cecilia, you got stuck with it.") or they would blow a sigh of relief and metally disengage ("Oh thank goodness it wasn't me!"). In both circumstances, I was left with speakers who felt nervous and group members who were no longer paying much attention.

Implement a Better Habit: *Prep the Speaker*

1. At the end of a collaborative task, regain the class's attention.

   Select a speaker from each group, and give a short amount of time for the group to "prep their speaker." It might sound like this:

   - *In one minute, person number three at each table will share out. For the next minute, please work as a team to make sure person number three is ready.*

   - *You have 30 seconds to prepare your speakers. Make sure they have lots of good ideas.*

   - *In a virtual setting, broadcast a message to all breakout rooms that states: "Person with shortest name will share out. You have 2 min to help him/her prepare."*

   - *Before my speakers share, I'll give you a few seconds to practice what you are going to say with your group.*

2. Ask each speaker to share out.

Why Is This Small Move Significant?

This small move is significant for both the speaker and the other group members. It benefits the speaker because it allows her to review the ideas that were discussed (or maybe focus on them for the first time if she wasn't paying attention). It also gives her a chance to orally rehearse her thinking before she speaks in front of the entire class, something which is particularly important for our English learners. Prepping her also benefits the members of her group. Encouraging the group to help the speaker prepare shifts the responsibility back to everyone in the group, allowing them to become a team rather than just a group of individuals. Instead of pointing and laughing at the selected student, group members support her, giving ideas and encouragement. Making this small move a habit absolutely creates a spirit of true collaboration.

Variations

• Encourage students to jot down ideas during collaboration so they have something to look at if they are called on.
• Encourage teammates (and the whole class) to validate each speaker's response with a gesture (silent cheer, "air" high five, etc.) and/or comments in the chat ("I agree, Marcus." "Our group mentioned that too!")

CLASSROOM EXAMPLE

Mrs. McDaris' World Cultures class is learning about the environmental issues Africa is facing. She has already shown them a short video clip that depicts some causes and effects of deforestation. At the end of the video she asks partners, who are labeled Partner A and Partner B, to discuss what they learned in the video. After a couple of minutes, she gets the class' attention and says, "I'll be calling on a few Partner As in 30 seconds. Before I do that, A's practice what you are going to say with your partner. B's help them out if they are stuck."

Plus Minus

Plus Minus is a small move for giving your students feedback after they collaborate in partnerships or in small groups. The idea is to give one plus, or positive reflection, and also one minus, something on which to improve for next time. This move is focused on increasing students' collaboration skills.

$+/-$

Challenge a Bad Habit

Most of the students I have taught did not arrive in my classroom with a well-developed skill set for engaging in academic conversations. I encountered a wide variety of challenges whenever I asked my students to talk to each other in class. Often one person takes over the entire conversation, or the group gets off task immediately, or no one wants to talk. Because of these challenges and others, I have seen teachers limit opportunities for collaboration. It becomes easier to plan less interactive ways for students to learn because the class is easier to manage.

Alternatively, for those of us who stubbornly continue to plan for students to talk to each other, we repeatedly run up against the same roadblocks. I am often so focused on the content of what students are saying that I am not really thinking about their communication skills. Most of my feedback is about what they are learning and rarely about how they are collaborating. The only time they get feedback on that is when the room feels loud and chaotic (and I lose my patience). Then I give plenty of rapid-fire feedback: "Everyone stop. I can't believe how loud it is in here. It is supposed to be voice level two, and you are

all yelling at each other. And look, right now seven of you are out of your seats, and Wyatt, why is your phone out? You guys, I am so frustrated. I thought you'd like the chance to talk to each other before you write your paragraph, but I can see we aren't able to do that. That's it! Everyone sit down and begin your assignment silently." My frustration, however, is unfair; I am irritated that they aren't doing what I expect, even though I have never taught them how to do it.

Implement a Better Habit: *Plus Minus*

1. When you give students an opportunity to talk within partnerships or small groups, actively monitor their conversations and behavior. In a virtual setting, you can focus in on specific breakout groups, "pop in" to all of them, as well as listen to any asynchronous talking tasks, like recording a Flipgrid response.

2. At the close of the collaboration time, tell the whole class one positive observation you made about their conversations (the "plus"), and share one observation that you would like to see them improve upon next time (the "minus").

3. Record your comments with the date and class period in a two-column journal.

DATE *November 2*	CLASS *3rd period*
plus	minus

4. The next time you give that class an opportunity to collaborate, open the two-column journal and review the plus and the minus from the last time. Encourage each group or partnership to focus on improving the "minus."

5. At the close of the collaboration time, repeat steps two and three.

It is important to limit the feedback to one plus and one minus, not many of each, which would no longer constitute a "small move."
**Keep your journal notes separate for each class.*

Why Is This Small Move Significant?

Often we ask students to talk to each other about academic content, but rarely do we think of "talk" as a skill we need to teach. We just tell them to discuss and hope for the best. This small move allows us to consistently teach students how to communicate more effectively in tiny little doses. When we give students a single and specific point of feedback about their attempts at collaboration immediately after they talk, we prompt their own reflection. When we give the same single and specific point of feedback right before they collaborate the next time, we advance their communication skills through immediate practice. The amount of feedback given is also significant. Several studies concerning the quantity of feedback given, specifically to English learners, found that feedback in excess of three responses resulted in diminished effectiveness (Havrenek, 2002; Daughty & Varela, 1998). Understandably, students begin to tune out after a while, so giving them a concise message matters.

Variations

• Rather than keeping a journal, each Plus/Minus can be displayed as an ongoing anchor chart that the class can see, acting as a visual reminder.
• Once this becomes a habit, let students give the plus and minus for their own group or for the class as a whole.
• Small groups can keep their own Plus/Minus journal.
• Use the Plus/Minus reflection for other areas besides collaboration (e.g. submitting work online, chat etiquette, workstation rotations, expectations for completing assignments, use of a specific online app, etc.).

CLASSROOM EXAMPLE

TEACHER: Ok everyone. Now that we have all finished reading both paired passages, I want you to discuss your annotations with your team. Your goal is to use both texts to come up with at least three inferences we can make about the Civil Rights movement. I'll give you about four minutes, and remember I am expecting each person to contribute. Ok, you can get started.

Students begin to discuss the two articles at their table groups. The teacher walks around to monitor their discussions. She helps one group who is arguing about who goes first, then she moves to another group where one student is practically shouting. As she makes her way to each group, she is thinking about what they are doing well and what needs improving. She realizes that lots of students are pointing to their passages when they are talking. She hears, "Like right here, where it says …" and "I highlighted this part." She also realizes that she has had to ask every table but one to lower their voices several times. After the four-minute timer goes off, she gets everyone's attention again.

TEACHER: Please wrap up your conversations in 5, 4, 3, 2, and 1. Before we discuss your inferences as a class, I wanted to tell you two things I noticed. First, I had to give cues about your voice level several times today. Next time you have table talk, let's focus on keeping your voices at a whisper. I also saw many of you referring back to your passage and actually touching the paragraph related to the idea you were sharing. That is so smart! It is important to support your ideas with evidence from the text.

The teacher quickly records that feedback in her Plus/Minus journal. It might look like this ➡

Fast-forward to a little later in the class period. After the entire class discusses their inferences, the teacher introduces the writing assignment and shows a sample under the document camera. She asks students to silently read the example to determine if it met all of the criteria for the assignment. Once students signal that they have finished reading and thinking about it, she gives them a chance to discuss their opinions with a partner.

TEACHER: Ok, I'd like for you to discuss with your partner whether you think this is a high-quality example of what to do on the assignment. Before you begin, remember I want you to continue to refer to the example to support your thinking, just like you did in the paired passages, and we also want to focus on keeping our voices at a whisper. You can begin.

CLASS *3rd period*		
date/topic	**plus**	**minus**
1/29 Civil Rights	referring to the text	voices too loud

03

Teacher Habits
That *Help Kids*
to *Think More*

What is one critical skill or
ability that you want your
students to gain this year?

When conducting professional development, I often begin each training by asking teachers this question: "What is one critical skill or ability that you want your students to gain this year?" Think about that for a second. If your kids learn nothing else from you, what is the one thing you want them to leave your classroom with? I almost always receive answers related to what I would call "life skills." Teachers say things like, "Problem solving skills," "I want them to really understand what they are reading," "To become independent learners," etc. The number one response I hear across all grades and content areas, however, is "critical thinking skills." We all want our students to be able to think deeply about what they are learning. We want them to connect ideas, analyze concepts, and apply what they have learned in new ways. In this chapter we will look at two significant targets that enable students to think more: engagement and self-assessment.

A variety of research supports the effectiveness of targeting engagement and student self-assessment. It makes intuitive sense (and research supports) that engaging students' brains is a direct pathway to learning (Skinner & Pitzer, 2012). That is, once engagement occurs, powerful learning outcomes often follow (National Research Council & Institute of Medicine, 2004). If students aren't engaged with the lesson, then it is usually the teacher, and not the students, doing the critical thinking. Similarly, if students do not self-assess their own understanding, the teacher remains in the driver's seat when it comes to thinking and learning. When students self-assess, they think about the quality of their own work rather than relying on their teacher as the sole source of evaluative judgements. (Andrade & Valtcheca, 2009). There are two goals for each of the small moves in this chapter:

✓ To ensure that students themselves are an active part of the lesson.

✓ To provide continuous opportunities for students to reflect on their own learning.

When both of those conditions occur, students do, in fact, think more!

SMALL MOVE	TARGET
• **Stop Fishing** • **Pronounce, Predict, Paraphrase** • **Pick a Number** • **Set a Purpose** • **Listen For …**	Engage students throughout the lesson
• **Solo Sandwich** • **Accurate Answer** • **Non-Example**	Prompt students to self-assess their learning

SMALL MOVE 3.1
Stop Fishing

"Fishing" in the classroom occurs when the teacher asks a question to no one in particular and then accepts the answers from the students who "bite." This small move is aimed at eliminating "fishing" and replacing it with a more strategic plan for calling on students to answer questions.

Challenge a Bad Habit

For the first few years of my teaching career, I "fished" for answers. I would ask questions to check for understanding by saying, "Can anyone tell me _____?" or "Who thinks they know _____?" Basically I would "cast out" each question hoping that someone would "bite." The only students who answered were my "shouter-outers." You know these kids — they are usually extroverted, and they like to participate. A colleague of mine, Carol Salva, calls them "professional answerers." I would accept their answers (which were almost always correct) because it enabled me to move through my lesson at an accelerated pace. There are two major problems with fishing for answers:

1. I am teaching to those who already know. By requesting volunteers to answer, I am only confirming that the students who probably entered my classroom knowing the content still know it.

2. I am training the rest of my class to disengage. I am not just allowing them to check out; I am *teaching* them to check out. When I fish for an answer, my actions are communicating that what I value is fast and correct, so if a student is not fast and correct, I do not have a place for them in my class.

Implement a Better Habit: *Stop Fishing*

1. Ask a question without beginning with "Can anyone tell me …" or "Who would like to explain …".

2. Manage "shouter-outers" if you have them. This might sound like:
   Everyone, let's put our hands down. I just want everyone to silently think about my question
   or
   Please stay muted and do not write anything in the chat. Just think about your answer for a couple of seconds.

3. Use a system for calling on students. Randomization and rotation strategies work great. Here are some examples of each on the following page.

RANDOMIZATION	ROTATION
• **Assign students numbers** and use 6-, 20-, or 25-sided dice to roll for a specific number	**Use the roster** • Beginning of roster, then last name on the roster, then second name, then second-to-last name
• **Tech tools** like Stick Pick, Class Dojo, and wheelofnames.com	• Call on every third name
• **Personal characteristics** like tallest at each table, color of shirt, favorite pizza topping	**Use class layout** • Call on students at each of the four corners and then work your way in toward the middle
• **Ask the previous student** who answered to select the next student to answer (this can involve tossing a stress ball or similar item)	• Call on the first person in every other row, then the last person in every other row, etc.

Why Is This Small Move Significant?

There are two primary reasons to stop fishing. The first is to increase engagement for everyone. If students know that there is a system in place where any student can be called on at any time, they focus more. When students are focused on tasks during instruction, learning increases (Schmoker, 2006). The second reason to eliminate fishing is to ensure that you have an equitable classroom. All learners deserve opportunities to think about and answer questions that vary in complexity, but without a system, such opportunities are only afforded to those who "bite." Even in classrooms where the teacher tries to call on everyone (without using a system), often our human nature takes over. We ask "stretch" questions to our highest-achieving kids, and because we know our struggling learners may lack confidence, we often end up only asking them questions we think they can answer. Such a practice only increases the gaps between learners rather than ensuring they all have equitable opportunities for learning.

CLASSROOM EXAMPLE

GRADE	INSTEAD OF... (NON-EXAMPLE)	TRY THIS... (EXAMPLE)
1st Grade ELAR	TEACHER: Who can tell me the setting of our story?	TEACHER: Let's all think about this: What is the setting of our story? *As a few students shout out say:* Shhh ... let's just think first. If you have a red shirt on, please stand up. Let's hear what you think about the setting of our story. *System: Randomization by shirt color*
High School Biology	TEACHER: Estefanie, thank you. You're right. Who can give me another example of an inherited trait? SOLOMON: The color of your eyes.	TEACHER: Estefanie, thank you. You're right. I'd like to hear two more examples of inherited traits. I'm going to use my roster. Let's see ... Justin and Jorge, can you each give us another example of an inherited trait? *System: Rotation through reverse alphabetical order on the roster*
8th Grade Math	TEACHER: How many variables are in this equation? A FEW STUDENTS: (shouting out) One! TEACHER: Yes that's correct. What do we do first to isolate it? SAME STUDENTS: Subtract! TEACHER: Exactly right.	TEACHER: Everyone, look at our equation. Without shouting out, show me with your fingers how many variables we have. *(Students show one finger.)* TEACHER: Great. We do have one. Now jot down on your dry erase board what you think we need to do to isolate it. *(As everyone writes, the teacher walks the room to see their answers.)* *System: Total written response*

Variations

- Get students involved. Assign a student to remind you to use your system.
- Ask all students to jot down their answers in a journal or in the chat.
- Ask students to share their answers with a partner.

Pronounce, Predict, Paraphrase

When introducing the objectives for the day, ask students to pronounce them, make predictions related to them, paraphrase them, or do something else with them. This small move is centered around engaging students in the first few minutes of class.

Challenge a Bad Habit

Often the beginning of class is dominated by the teacher. When I started teaching, I always began lessons by introducing the objectives for the day. I'd walk over to my chalkboard (Yes, I'm that old!) and stand by where I'd written the goals for the lesson and class agenda. Then I'd read it to my students, adding in any explanations as necessary. This usually took two to three minutes. Then I'd walk back toward the middle of the room and begin the lesson, which usually resulted in another five to 20 minutes of me talking. Even though I considered myself an energetic and engaging teacher, I am sure the majority of my students perceived me as sounding like Charlie Brown's teacher: "Wah wah, wah wah, wah wah."

Implement a Better Habit:
Pronounce, Predict, Paraphrase

1. Post objectives.
2. As you introduce them, ask students to pronounce, predict, paraphrase, or do something else with them. Here are some examples:
   • Read them out loud chorally, to a partner, or silently.
   • Select any word(s) they don't know.
   • Make a prediction about what they will learn today.
   • Paraphrase what the objective means to their partners.
   • Pick the key words they think are most important.
   • Rate their current level of understanding of the objective on a scale of one to five.
3. Periodically refer back to the objectives throughout the lesson, and use them as part of a wrap-up.

Why Is This Small Move Significant?

The primary benefit of asking students to engage with the objectives is the "engage" part. Many of our students enter our classrooms (F2F or virtual) preoccupied. A kindergartener might be focused on another kid's light-up shoes. A seventh grader might be upset because she received a mean text from a friend. A junior in high school might be exhausted because he worked until midnight and has your class first period. All of those distractions remain intact until each of these students is required to do something other than just listen to the teacher. This small move disrupts any distractions and prompts students to check in to the lesson. Asking students to do something with the objectives also promotes their understanding and increases their ability to explain the learning goal for the lesson (Frey, Fisher, & Nelson, 2013). Another benefit of asking students to pronounce, predict, paraphrase, or identify components of the objectives is that you gain information about students' levels of understanding of the content immediately; formative assessment begins at the very beginning of class.

CLASSROOM EXAMPLE

TEACHER: Good morning everyone. I'd like for everyone to silently read our goals for today. Your job is to type what you think the 3 most important words are into the chat. There is no right or wrong answer, and you can send it just to me or to everyone.

CONTENT OBJECTIVE

- I will identify the properties of similar triangles by labeling and explaining each property on my paper.

LANGUAGE OBJECTIVE

- I will orally explain my work to my partner using:

  One property of similar triangles is...

Today's terms: property, similar

TEACHER: Ok boys and girls, let's read our objective all together. Look where my pointer is. *(All students chorally read the goals with the teacher.)*

CONTENT OBJECTIVE

- I will summarize *The Three Little Pigs* by writing the beginning, middle, and end in my journal.

LANGUAGE OBJECTIVE

I will listen carefully so I can retell the story to my partner.

Variations

- Apply *Pronounce, Predict, Paraphrase* in other lesson components. For example, do students have to do something besides listen when you are lecturing, modeling, delivering a mini lesson, or demonstrating a skill?
- In a virtual setting, ask students to predict, paraphrase, or pick important words and record them in the chat.

Pick a Number

In this small move, instead of just asking a question, the teacher also picks a number for how many different responses she'd like students to generate. This move is particularly supportive during partner or small-group talk to help students sustain and extend discussion.

Challenge a Bad Habit

Whenever I gave my students a writing assignment, the first question out of their mouths was, "How long does it have to be?" In other words, what many of them often wanted to know was how much work they actually had to do. When we ask students to orally discuss content, they often operate from the same mentality: finish as quickly as possible. Once they have an answer, they stop thinking about and discussing the topic. Because they have at least one answer, they are now free to think about and/or discuss other things (almost never related to the lesson). Telling students directly that you are expecting more than one answer changes the way students talk about what they are learning.

Implement a Better Habit: *Pick a Number*

1. Ask an open-ended question that you'd like students to discuss.
2. Challenge students to generate a minimum number of responses. You might say something like this after asking the question:

See if you can jot down at least two answers.

I can think of five different answers. I'd like you and your partner to come up with at least three.

Let's see which breakout room can generate the highest number of different ways to answer this question. Your minimum goal is four answers.

Why Is This Small Move Significant?

Educational research has shown that students' engagement in collaborative inquiry has a positive effect on their knowledge construction (Beach & Myers, 2001; Haneda & Wells, 2008). Challenging students to "dig deeper" by giving them a quantifiable goal supports such inquiry. When we pick a number, we shift student focus from thinking about the "right" answer to thinking about all possible answers. In most student discussions, the most "knowing" and most extroverted students speak first, and they usually have a correct answer. By stating that you are expecting more than that, you are creating a space for other students who may need more processing time to share their thinking.

CLASSROOM EXAMPLE

GRADE	TRY THIS... (EXAMPLE)
2nd Grade ELAR	How can you tell if you selected a "just right" book from the library? See if you and your partner can think of three different ways. You can record those on your jamboard.
8th Grade U.S. History	With your group, I'd like for you to identify the differences between the patriot perspective and the loyalist perspective. I'd like for you to discuss more than the obvious one or two differences. See if you can generate at least five.
6th Grade Math	Compare the way you solved the problem with your partner. Was it the same or different? Either way, see if together you can use at least one additional strategy for solving the problem.

Variations

- Periodically make discussion a competition: Which group/partnership can create the most responses?
- Add a visual/concrete element to discussions. For example, groups can stack a lego for each new idea or move an object from one basket to another for each new idea.

Set a Purpose

In this small move, the teacher clearly gives students a purpose for reading. The goal is to increase student focus and comprehension.

Challenge a Bad Habit

When I taught using the Reader's Workshop model in upper elementary, I'd often give each small group a reading assignment to complete on their own. Let's say one of my groups was reading *The Watsons Go to Birmingham -1963*, by Christopher Paul Curtis (1995). During small-group time that day, we did a close reading looking for figurative language in chapter 3. At the end of the small-group session, I'd say something like, "Great work today. I'll see you all again in two days. Please read up to chapter 5, and then we'll discuss it."

Fast forward two days. I'd meet with that group again with the plan to continue to analyze how and why the author used figurative language. After ensuring everyone did the assigned reading, I'd begin with something like, "Ok, last time we were identifying various types of figurative language that the author used. What examples of figurative language did you find when you were reading?" My students' responses were either blank stares, shoulder shrugs, or frantic scans through the pages of their books. None of them had noticed any figurative language. Here's the thing: I never told them to look for figurative language. I knew what my plan for that assigned reading was, but I never let them in on the "secret." Because I did not give them

a purpose for the reading, I was never able to accomplish the learning target. We spent the entire time rereading simply to find examples rather than analyzing examples. Imagine what would have happened if, when I closed the first day, I had said, "Great work today. I'll see you all again in two days. Please read up to chapter 5, looking for examples of figurative language. While you read, please record at least three examples in your journals. We will discuss those when we meet again." Setting the purpose would have allowed my students and me to achieve much more.

Implement a Better Habit: *Set a Purpose*

1. Preview the text to determine the purpose for reading it.
2. Explicitly tell your students the purpose.
3. Ask students to read for that stated purpose.

Why Is This Small Move Significant?

Setting a purpose for reading is a foundational component of effective reading instruction (Morgan et al., 2013; Guccione, 2011; Taylor & Neshiem, 2000). Without a purpose, students' comprehension can get lost or veer off course. Setting a purpose for reading focuses readers, which is particularly significant for struggling or apathetic students. The purpose makes the reading task more manageable, giving them a single goal to guide their thinking. Students also begin to understand that the way they read in social studies, for example, might require a different set of knowledge and strategies than the way they read in a math class (Botzokies et al., 2014). It also benefits speed readers who tend to race through the text. With a purpose, these students slow down to accomplish the reading goal rather than just "finishing" the text.

CLASSROOM EXAMPLE

Setting a purpose is not limited to just reading. As shown in these examples, we can set the purpose for all student tasks.

CHEMISTRY

We are going to watch a video clip where you will see several types of reactions. I want you to watch and think about whether each reaction is exothermic or endothermic. Check your notes to confirm your thinking. After each one I'll pause the video and we will vote whether it was exothermic or endothermic.

MATH

Before we solve the equation, let's slow down and reread the word problem. Your purpose for reading is to find any signal words that will help us determine which operation we will use.

PRINCIPLES OF BUSINESS

This article is all about Nike's™ current status. Your purpose for reading is to identify at least two factors that are affecting Nike's profits.

P.E.

I'm going to demonstrate the proper technique for a bench press. Your main purpose is to notice my wrists and elbows as I press. Pay extra attention to how Coach Schmidt and I spot each other when we use the heavier set of weights.

Variations

- Record the purpose for reading on the text itself so that students see it while reading.

- Help students set their own purposes for reading. Directing them to any titles, subheadings, and pictures will help. Prediction Path (Zweirs, 2011) is a great activity for this.

most color change reaction and are used to support the ......

Here are the names of some of the common acids and bases and the formulas associated with them.

Formulas of Binary Acids

A binary compound consists of two elements. Binary acids have the prefix *hydro* in front of the full name of the nonmetallic element. They have the ending *-ic*. Examples include hydrochloric, and hydrofluoric acid includes:

Hydrofluoric Acid – HF

Hydrochloric Acid – HCl

Hydrobromic Acid – HBr

Hydroiodic Acid – HI

Hydro sulfuric Acid – H_2S

Hydro cyanic acid – HCN

Purpose:
Find 3 differences between Binary Aci + Ternary Acids

Formulas of Ternary Acids

...nary acids commonly contain hydrogen, a nonmetal, and oxygen.

...name of the most common form of the acid consists of the nonmetal root ...e with the -ic ending. The acid containing one less oxygen atom than the common form is designated by the -ous ending. An acid containing one less ...n atom than the -ous acid has the prefix *hypo*- and the -ous ending. The ...ntaining one more oxygen than the most common acid has the *per*- prefix ...- -ic ending.

...cid – $HNO3$ Nitrous Acid – $HNO2$

...rous Acid – HClO   Chlorous Acid – $HClO2$ Chloric Acid – $HClO3$
...Acid – $HClO4$

...d – $H2SO4$ Sulfurous Acid – $H2SO3$

SMALL MOVE 3.5
Listen For …

Active listening is what this small move is all about. The teacher gives students a purpose for listening along with some form of accountable output.

Challenge a Bad Habit

Students spend the majority of their school days listening; they listen to their teachers, they listen to other students, they listen to video clips and other online resources. However, how do we *really* know if they are listening? Certainly there are some tell-tale signs, like making eye contact with the speaker or nodding in agreement, but those can easily be faked. Young students might appear to be "with you" when they are really daydreaming about being on the playground. Older students might be nodding at you at appropriate times to indicate they are listening, when in reality they have figured out to nod back at you when your inflection goes up or when you look directly at them. They aren't actually listening, they are just responding to your non-verbal cues while thinking about their personal lives outside of school. When we give students a specific purpose for listening and then immediately follow the listening task with some form of accountable response, we diminish "fake listening" and increase each student's focus.

Implement a Better Habit: *Listen For…*

1. During receptive tasks (listening to a mini-lesson, watching a video clip, or listening during group collaboration), give students a purpose for listening.

2. Ask students to demonstrate that they have been listening by using some form of output (written, oral, or gesture).

Why Is This Small Move Significant?

When students are tasked with a specific listening goal, we are increasing their attention to what they are learning. When we add to that goal a concrete way for each of them to demonstrate what they understood from listening, we are also increasing each student's ownership over their own learning (Johnson, 2011). When implementing *Listen For…* becomes a habit, it results in students engaging at a much higher level because they know that at any point during instruction they may be asked to retell, further process, or extend their understanding of the content being taught. They transition from being passive receivers of knowledge to active users of that knowledge.

CLASSROOM EXAMPLE

4th Grade:

TEACHER: I'd like all the number twos to stand up. Each of you will share out one of the signal words that your team discussed using our sentence stem. Everyone else, we need to listen to see if they have the same idea that your team discussed or a different one. If they share something your team talked about also, please snap your fingers above your head. If they share an idea that is different from your team's ideas, please tap on the table with two fingers. Let's practice. Show me what you do if their idea is different from yours. *(Students tap with two fingers on the table.)*

Output is the gesture.

9th Grade:

TEACHER: We're going to take a few notes today, but I don't want anyone copying. While I explain each slide, I am looking for you to listen and follow along without writing anything. At the end of each slide, I'm going to black out the screen and then give you a couple of minutes to jot down the key points. It is important that you listen carefully so that your notes can be high quality.

Output is writing.

Band:

TEACHER: I'm going to play a few sections of our latest piece. After each section you and your partner are going to discuss the tone of each one. It'll sound like this: "I would describe the tone as _____ because ..."

Output is oral.

Variations

- During partner or group conversations, ask the speaker to "retell, then add." Students should restate or paraphrase what they heard the last speaker say before they add their own thinking.
- For extended periods of listening (e.g., a 15-minute mini-lesson or an eight-minute video), chunk the listening task. Give mini purposes every few minutes to help maintain student focus.

SMALL MOVE 3.6
Solo Sandwich

In this move, the teacher gives students individual (solo) processing time before and after collaborative tasks. This extra processing time helps "hold together" the learning done in the collaborative thinking time, much like the way bread holds together a

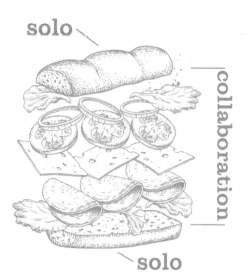

solo

collaboration

solo

Challenge a Bad Habit

Today's face-to-face and virtual classrooms are full of collaborative tasks, and flexible grouping. Because students spend a large amount of instructional time working with others, it can be challenging to get an accurate check on each student's individual understanding. Additionally, the lines between each student's own thinking and his or her partner's thinking often get blurred. I know I have had students who thought they completely understood a given standard because all of the group tasks made sense to them. However, when they were individually held accountable on a graded assignment, they were not nearly as successful. While they had actively participated in the collaborative tasks, they had in effect "hitchhiked" on the thinking of their peers, agreeing with other ideas but not generating their own. If we create a space immediately before and after collaborative tasks for students to think on their own, we not only increase the quality of the collaboration but we also train our students to self-assess their own understanding, which in turn increases engagement at higher levels of cognition.

Implement a Better Habit:
Solo Sandwich

1. Pose the question, thinking task, or assignment to the entire class.
2. Give students time to individually process the presented material. This can be achieved by having students jot down their thinking on paper or possibly just show a total response signal when they are finished thinking. In a virtual setting, this can be done asynchronously as well.
3. Give students a structured opportunity to collaborate (e.g., discuss the question, problem solve the task, or complete the assignment).
4. Give students time to individually assess their understanding (e.g,. write down their thinking, complete a similar problem on their own, or rate their current understanding with a number or gesture). In a virtual setting, this can be done asynchronously as well.

Why Is This Small Move Significant?

When we make the Solo Sandwich a habit in class, students are constantly given opportunities to reflect on their own learning. During every solo task, they are thinking critically and self-assessing. Research indicates that students who engage in well-designed self-assessment tasks experience a deep understanding of content, value their educational experiences, and actively participate in activities (Munns & Woodard, 2006). You can see how this makes sense. Imagine a student who, when asked to jot down his thoughts before talking to his team, realizes (through self-assessment) that he doesn't understand the content. This act of self-assessment will prompt him to pay much closer attention to the group discussion, thus increasing both his content knowledge and active engagement.

Another reason this small move is significant is that it increases each student's individual accountability. For each opportunity to think collaboratively, students have two opportunities to think all by themselves.

Variations

- Giving "solo" time before and after every collaboration may not be necessary, especially once students are acclimated to being held individually accountable in a consistent manner.
- A reading task could replace or precede the first individual thinking time. For example, students read a word problem on their own (solo), then discuss it (collaborative), then solve it on their own (solo).
- In a virtual setting, we can often increase the "solo" time by giving students asynchronous tasks before and after synchronous collaboration. This is particularly helpful for students who might need more time to process.

CLASSROOM EXAMPLE

GRADE	SOLO	COLLABORATIVE	SOLO
Kindergarten Science	"Boys and girls, let's all think about how we can describe the weather outside. Everyone, draw your idea on your dry erase board."	"I'm going to ask you to tell your partner about what you drew. Describe the weather to your partner. Partner A goes first." *Partners discuss the weather.* *Teacher calls on a few students to describe the weather and records those responses on an anchor chart.*	"We have some good ideas on our chart. Now let's all write about today's weather. Here is our stem: 'Today's weather is ....' You can use one of the ideas from our chart or your own." *Students write about the weather using the provided sentence stem.*
Middle School ELAR	"For your warm-up, please read the poem and try to find at least two examples of figurative language. Record those in your digital interactive journal and think about why the author included them."	"With your breakout room, please share the examples of figurative language you found. Also use the following stem to discuss each one: 'I think the author included _____ because ...'" "I'd like you to share in reverse order: D's, then C's, then B's, then A's."	"Pick one example of figurative language from the poem. In your digital interactive notebook, record your thinking about it using our stem: 'I think the author included _____ because ...'"
High School Chemistry	*After introducing the lab, the teacher asks students to record their hypotheses.*	*Before starting the lab, partners discuss their hypotheses to determine if they were the same or different.* *Partners conduct the lab.* *Partners discuss the outcomes of the lab to determine whether their hypotheses were correct.*	*Students write their lab reports individually, using a template that the teacher provided.*

Accurate Answer

Accurate Answer **is a small move for responding to students when they give an incorrect answer to a question at the knowledge or comprehension level during class. Not every question we ask is open-ended or intended to provoke discussion. Sometimes we ask questions to quickly assess whether students understand or remember something we have taught. This small move provides an approach, grounded in research, for handling incorrect answers.**

Challenge a Bad Habit

When students give us a correct answer, we usually reply with a direct response, saying "You're right," or "That's correct." When students give us an incorrect answer, however, we often give a vague reply. Think about what you say to a student who gives a wrong answer. I know my response often sounds something like this: "I can tell you're thinking, but who else has an idea?" Or I might say, "Ok, that was a good try. Let's see … Frankie, what do you think?" Those comments are intended to encourage my students and show them that I appreciate their participation, but unfortunately, they do not help them learn. Responding to incorrect answers with comments like the ones above creates confusion for both the student who gave the incorrect answer and for the rest of the class. Because part of the response was positive ("I can tell you're thinking"), students might interpret the answer as correct, solidifying misinformation. Even if the student understood from your reply that the answer was in fact incorrect, you are relying on the next student ("Who else has an idea?") to provide accurate information,

which may or may not happen. It is all too common for teachers to have to call on several students before getting an accurate response.

Implement a Better Habit:
Accurate Answer

If the student's answer is incorrect, reply with an accurate answer.

What does the accurate answer include? There are three parts to this small move:

1. Identify the answer as incorrect (or partially incorrect if applicable). This might sound harsh, but learning occurs when they find out 1) that their response was wrong and 2) why it was wrong. This is challenging for many of us because we do not want to embarrass or upset students. I recommend creating a standard phrase that you feel comfortable with and using it over and over. For example, "Actually that isn't correct. Let me explain …" or "That is not quite right. The correct answer is _____ because …"

2. Teach the correct answer. You are the

expert in the room, and you are the most qualified person to help the students learn and clarify their understanding. Explain why the incorrect answer is wrong and why the correct answer is right in a direct and brief manner.

3. Ask a follow-up question based on the correct information you just gave. It could be identical to the original question or a variation or extension of it. This allows the student(s) to immediately apply the feedback you just gave in context.

Why Is This Small Move Significant?

Robert Marzano et al. (2001) refers to this as "corrective" feedback (p. 96). His research demonstrates that students learn and achieve more when the feedback they receive explains what was inaccurate and what was accurate (if anything) about their response. Providing an accurate answer immediately following confusion is also more efficient. Instead of spending minutes hearing incorrect or strange responses, all students receive solid information and then have time to continue to apply it or move on. Asking the follow-up question also teaches students to use the feedback they receive. "The process of intentionally implementing feedback is likely to keep people (students) in a practice state of increased consciousness and thus steeper improvement" (Lemov et al., 2012, p. 110).

Variations:

Instead of giving the correct answer immediately, give students additional processing time or direct them to a resource to find the correct answer. For example, "That's not quite right. Everyone, look back at the notes you just took. See if you can find the right answer."

CLASSROOM EXAMPLE

Non-example

TEACHER: What do we call the person who draws all the pictures in books?

Some hands go up.

TEACHER: Franklin?

FRANKLIN: The artist?

TEACHER: Close, they are a kind of artist. Serena, what do you think?

SERENA: The author!

TEACHER: That is a good guess, they are important, too. Who can help me, though? What is the name of the person who draws the pictures?

Example

TEACHER: What do we call the person who draws all the pictures in books?

TEACHER: Franklin?

FRANKLIN: The artist?

TEACHER: Actually this person is called the illustrator. Let's all say that.

CLASS: Illustrator.

TEACHER: Illustrators are artists for books. So Franklin, what do we call the person who draws the pictures?

FRANKLIN: The person who draws pictures is the illustrator.

Non-Example

In this small move, the teacher models for the students both what to do and what *not* to do in a given task.

Challenge a Bad Habit

I have had countless teaching experiences where I've thought I did a pretty good job modeling the given task for students, and yet they were unsuccessful. I've done think alouds and given step-by-step directions while students watched me model how to complete the work. However, what they were able to produce was low quality and/or incorrect. Usually, the errors in the task were common among many of my students. For example, in a science lab report, the majority of my students might have forgotten to label the units for their calculations (inches, kilograms, feet per second, etc.) even though the sample lab report I'd modeled had all units labeled. Providing a non-example helps mitigate those challenges. If, in addition to the high quality sample, I also show a lab report that is missing all units and draw their attention to that difference in the two samples, I am dramatically increasing the likelihood that students will include units in their reports.

Implement a Better Habit: *Non-Example*

1. Explain/model the expectation (example).
2. Explain/model the opposite of the expectation (non-example).
3. Conduct a brief discussion of the differences between the two samples, possibly even charting those ideas so students can refer back to them while completing the assignment themselves.

Why Is This Small Move Significant?

Providing both an example and a non-example gives students a range of expectations and more explicit criteria. The example and non-example serve as the "bookends" demonstrating the range of student work that is typically completed. Often the lack of quality in the non-example highlights the key components of the high-quality example, making what you are looking for more clear to your students. This move gives our students opportunities to hone their inductive learning skills, which encourages them to adopt a deeper approach to learning (Prince & Felder, 2007). Showing students the non-example also allows you to provide corrective feedback before students even make any errors. In other words, your non-example can specifically target the errors you know or anticipate your students will make.

CLASSROOM EXAMPLE

High School U.S. History

Task: Write a paragraph explaining some of the causes of the Great Depression.

Before assigning the task, the teacher shows students both the non-example and the example. Starting with the non-example, the teacher leads a discussion about what is lacking in the sample. Next the class looks at the example and discusses what is effective in that sample.

○ *Non- Example*

In 1929 the Stock Market crashed. Everyone was doing good before that but then it crashed. That was a bad day. Problem with the banks and World War 1 made it bad too. Lots of people lost their jobs and no one could get their money. People were hungry and mad at The Fed. Everyone was losing their houses and their careers, and they couldn't find any new jobs.

Example

○ *Some of the causes of the Great Depression include the stock market crash of 1929, the failure of the banking system, and also the policies of the Federal Reserve System (the FED). First, on October 29, 1929, the stock market crashed, making shares that people owned virtually worthless. Once this happened, everyone panicked. They went to their banks to try to get all of their money out of their accounts. The banks didn't have enough cash to give to everyone, so they closed. Most people found themselves without money and without work. The FED policies also contributed to the Great Depression. One policy was that they increased interest rates between 1928 and 1929. This caused people to spend less, which contributed to the rapid drop in the stock market. The FED also did not do anything to prevent or stop the banking crisis in the*
○ *years that followed the crash. They could have done something but did not, which made the Great Depression last for many years after the crash.*

CLASSROOM EXAMPLE

4th Grad ELAR
Task: Talk with your table groups about which statements in the article are facts and which are opinions.

Before asking table groups to start the discussion, the teacher might provide verbal examples and non-examples such as the following:

 *Example*

> "When you discuss, I am listening for each of your groups to generate lots of ideas. I also want everyone to participate. Let's take this group right here: Jamika, Bobby, Melissa, and Eddie should all give their ideas and take turns."

 Non-example

> "Here is what I don't want to hear or see: Jamika shows her article to her tablemates and says, 'Look these are all the facts. I highlighted them in blue, and I put the opinions in yellow,' and then Eddie says, 'Cool let me see that,' and then they all copy her highlighting while Bobby says, 'So did you see what was for lunch today? What is it? Nuggets or pizza? I can't remember.'"

Variations

- Highlighting non-examples for behaviors (how to greet a guest to the classroom) and/or non-academic tasks (how to transition from one workstation to another) are also really helpful.
- Larry Ferlazzo and Katie Hull Sypnieski (2018) have specific graphics and examples for how a non-example might look for helping students understand grammar structures as well as improve their writing.

Teacher Habits That *Help Kids* to *Achieve More*

The small moves in this chapter are intended to help students "achieve more" of the curriculum goals and the standards for any given grade and discipline.

Achievement can be valued and interpreted in a wide variety of ways, so I'd like to more narrowly define achievement as the ability for students to learn the academic content that you have taught them. The small moves in this chapter are intended, therefore, to help students "achieve more" of the curriculum goals and the standards for any given grade and discipline. Sometimes our passion for and deep knowledge of our content can actually get in the way of our students' learning. When we are experts of our content areas, sometimes we think it is easy to walk in and just start teaching. For some students (those who share our passion for the topic), this might work. However, for most of our students to really understand the information and to "achieve more," we also need to think about three additional considerations: the classroom environment, the way we deliver the content, and how we use instructional time.

A threatening learning environment can keep the brain from accessing and storing information and lower the ability to use higher-level thinking (Jensen, 2008). Conversely, if students feel safe and comfortable in their learning environment, they are far more likely to acquire new information because their brains are at ease. The first two small moves in this chapter focus on just that.

The second group of small moves centers around delivering the content in a more user-friendly and visual way, drawing attention to non-linguistic supports and intentionally planning memorable stories to connect to our lessons.

The final group of small moves is intended to help each of us become more efficient in the way we teach. Teaching with greater precision allows students to focus more directly on the content being taught, which in turn enables them to achieve more.

SMALL MOVE	TARGET
• Smile • Public Success	Creating a safe and comfortable learning environment
• Color-Code • Touch to Teach • Tell a Story	Teaching in a more visual and memorable way
• Timer • Fewest Words Possible • Walk With Intention	Teaching more efficiently

Smile

This self-explanatory small move can immediately improve almost anything during the school day.

Challenge a Bad Habit

When I am driving, my daughters often ask me, "Mom, what's wrong?" or "Is everything ok?" I'm caught off guard by those questions because, usually, nothing is wrong. I think, "I'm actually in a good mood. Why would they think that?" The answer is my face. They look at my face in the rearview mirror, and it does not look happy. I really don't like driving. I tend to worry that all the other drivers around me will do something wrong, and I generally stress out. It turns out my "driving face" looks like this:

What does your "teaching face" look like? Does it change from the first lesson of the day to the last? Does it look the same on Monday as it does on Friday? What about in May? How does your "teaching face" look in the middle of testing or the week grades are due? Our facial expression is the first and most authentic way we communicate with our students. It sets the tone for all learning.

Implement a Better Habit: *Smile*

1. Smile.
2. Repeat step one as much as possible.

Why Is This Small Move Significant?

"Make yourself so happy that when others look at you, they become happy too." A friend posted this Yogi Bhajan quote on Facebook, and I appreciate this sentiment. Our students face many challenges, but if they can rely on our joy (as evidenced in a real smile), they will undoubtedly become more joyful. Your reward for making smiling a habit in your classroom will be a happier classroom. Interestingly, even if you aren't feeling particularly joyful, choosing to smile has the same effect as doing so naturally. Researchers found that both spontaneous and manipulated smiles activate the part of the brain that is associated with positive emotions (Ekman & Davidson, 1993). In other words, a "forced" smile can lead to a real one because of your brain chemistry.

CLASSROOM EXAMPLE

LaKeysha Brown
1st Grade Teacher
Haynes Northwest Academy
Wichita Falls ISD

Janet Hughes
5th Grade Science
Booker T. Washington
Elementary

Sharon (Sherry) Fisher
Pre-K Teacher
Haynes Northwest Academy

Michael A. Mitchell
6th Grade Science
Kirby Middle School
Wichita Falls ISD

Variations

- Laugh.
- Give high fives, fist bumps, and side hugs.
- Pick out a student in each class who is usually happy. Make a mental link so that, when you see that student, you smile at the class.
- Compliment students when they are being joyful.
- If a student is not happy, acknowledge that while helping them to problem solve.
- If teaching virtually, put a reminder to smile next to the camera on your computer. It might look like this ⟶
- If you are wearing a mask, be sure to smile anyway. Students can "read" our expressions even if they only see our eyes.

Public Success

In this move, teachers ensure the success of each student who is called upon to participate publicly (with other students watching). More specifically, when you call on a student to answer a question, be deliberate in your feedback and actions to ensure that your student experiences success before moving on.

Challenge a Bad Habit

Doesn't everyone want to be successful? I know I do! I spend the majority of my time trying to be better ... a better parent, a better friend, a better employee, and certainly a better teacher. In fact, I can honestly say I have never met anyone who likes to fail. I have, however, encountered many students who, because of their previous school experiences, begin to expect failure. I see it in a defeated look, in the eye roll of my most apathetic student, and in the sea of black boxes where my online students' faces should be. These students do not like being called on in either a face-to-face (F2F) or virtual class because they don't know the answer or maybe because they lack confidence. Either way, they expect that they will be wrong. Compounding their uneasiness is the knowledge that all of their peers will be watching them as they fail.

What if instead, every student (especially our most struggling and disengaged) experienced an alternative reaction to being called upon? What if they automatically expected success instead of failure? Can you imagine the transformative effect this could have on our students? Imagine, for example, that you are teaching an economics lesson concurrently to F2F and virtual students. Your students, both "roomies" and "zoomies" have been learning about the differences among five industries (primary, secondary, tertiary, quaternary, and quinary). To check student understanding you ask, "Based on your notes, which type of industry are hotels and resorts? And why would they be classified that way?" You give students a few seconds to think about it and then call on Rosa. She is learning remotely and does not have her camera turned on, but you are pretty sure she is there because she has been completing the work throughout the class on a Google doc that you can see. You encourage her privately in the chat, but after a few long seconds, her response in the chat is, "I don't know." What would you do as her teacher? Would you tell her, "That's ok," and then ask, "Can anyone help Rosa out?" Would you give her the answer, saying, "Rosa, hotels are a tertiary industry because they provide a service to immediate customers." Would you say, "Come on Rosa. I know you remember this from yesterday." In each of the above responses, did Rosa experience success? I would argue no. She was unable to respond, passed over (responses one and two), and possibly embarrassed (response three). Odds are, she's feeling less confident and less safe than she did when class began. So how do you create an experience of public success for Rosa? What can you do when she is hesitant or unsure of the answer? There are many ways to treat this situation so that Rosa is successful at the end of the interaction. Here are a few ways to ensure her public success (and the success of any other student who is selected to answer a question):

Implement a Better Habit: *Public Success*

When you call on a student who is unsure or not responding, you can do the following:

1. Give a clue, tip, or hint, and reask the question.
2. Direct all students to a resource that can help while checking in privately with the first student.
3. Give the student an opportunity to collaborate with peers, and then come back to her.

Why Is This Small Move Significant?

One great way each of us can create "avenues for success" in our classrooms is through the type of feedback we offer. When interacting with students in a small-group or whole-group setting, try focusing on public success. The idea is to make sure that each time the "spotlight" is shined on a particular student, that student leaves the exchange having experienced success. Every student wants to be correct. Think about yourself as a student: if you get called on and answer correctly, you feel good. It makes you feel smart and increases the likelihood that you'll participate

in the future. Simply put, success generates motivation. Once students experience success, they will undoubtedly want more, which will increase their participation and engagement.

Variations

• Make pronunciation practice and choral response a regular habit in your classroom. This is particularly helpful for ensuring the success of our English learners who are being exposed to huge volumes of new words. Even when they understand the meaning of new vocabulary, our students are often reticent to use it because they aren't sure how to say it. *Virtual students can stay muted while practicing to further minimize any reluctance.

• During collaborative tasks, ask students to share something they learned from their partner or something their partner did really well. Sharing others' ideas removes some of the pressure students may feel when sharing their own thinking. (For more details see *Anyone's Idea*, p. 35.)

• When monitoring students, share specific things you observe that are positive. Examples might sound like, "When I joined break out room 4, I heard all three members use the sentence stem that I gave you. Excellent job!" or "As I'm walking around, I notice that Davis and Mareka both remembered to label the units on their coordinate grid. Attention to details like that is important." Comments like this indirectly promote the success of all learners in the class as they each quickly check to see if they labeled their units.

CLASSROOM EXAMPLE

Each example below highlights one of the ways to respond to Rosa, the student from the previous description.

GIVE A CLUE, TIP, OR HINT, AND RE-ASK THE QUESTION:

When Rosa types "I don't know" give her some help and then reask the question, offering a sentence stem to reduce her anxiety and increase language production. "Rosa, I'm going to put our chart back up on my screen. *(Point to it using your cursor)*. Hotels and resorts provide a service to their customers, so which industry on our chart shows that? Here's how you can answer: 'The industry that includes hotels and resorts is...' "

DIRECT ALL STUDENTS TO A RESOURCE THAT CAN HELP WHILE CHECKING IN PRIVATELY WITH THE FIRST STUDENT:

Upon seeing Rosa's "I don't know" response in the chat, you can prompt her to get her own help, saying, "Everyone take a couple of minutes to find your chart from yesterday, and reread it. It should be in the first folder. Think about where hotels would fit." As everyone rereads their notes, you can quickly type a private response to her with some one-on-one help. Rather than chatting to everyone, select just Rosa's name. You can say something like, "I know this is really intimidating, but I'm confident in your ability to answer the question. If you're really not sure, you can choose to ask a friend for help. In just a moment I'm going to unmute and ask you to either answer or choose someone to offer an idea. After they talk, you'll need to say you agree or disagree and why. I'm proud of you for trying - I know it's scary!" *Tip: Copying the text will allow you to quickly send the same message to other students if they feel intimidated or reluctant about sharing their thoughts.*

GIVE THE STUDENT AN OPPORTUNITY TO COLLABORATE WITH PEERS:

Asking all students to be logged into the virtual platform allows you to put students in virtual "break out" rooms even if they are physically in class. In this case, each small group will likely consist of a combination of students who are F2F and virtual. This structure can be very helpful when Rosa feels unsure, because you can give her (and the rest of the class) an opportunity to quickly collaborate with peers, by saying, "Everyone, check in with your small groups. See if together you guys can agree on which industry includes hotels and resorts." Just like the previous example, this creates time for you to quickly provide support to Rosa's breakout group before bringing the entire class back together.

In each of the scenarios above, when you come back to Rosa, she has an answer that she can feel good about. When she responds with the class observing, she will experience public success. This interaction will likely increase her motivation to participate in the future because of the positive emotion attached to her experience.

Color-Code

Color-Code is a small move where teachers color-code their teaching objectives, goals, and agendas based on various criteria. The goal is to use a different color to identify certain types of words, thus visually highlighting them for students.

Why Make Color-Coding a Habit?

Does your campus have a newsletter? When I began teaching, I would receive them on salmon-colored paper in my teacher mailbox in the workroom. Years later on, I'd receive them electronically in my inbox. In both cases, the format of the newsletter never changed — same sections, same fonts, one color. Over time I found that I stopped reading them. The same situation often occurs in our classrooms with our teaching objectives. Whether they are recorded on one side of the dry erase board or presented as the first slide in a presentation, they are usually displayed the same way, in the same color (often black) every day. Over time students stop paying attention to them because of the repetitive and "plain" nature of how they are displayed. Even when teachers introduce the lesson goals, students are left without a way to visually determine what is important.

Implement a Better Habit: *Color-Code*

1. Post objectives for each lesson according to your campus and district expectations. Note: Depending on your campus or district, these may be called learning targets, student expectations, "I will/We will" statements, content and language objectives, etc.
2. Color-code the words based upon what you'd like students to notice. (See examples on p. 72.) Most often I use three colors, with each color representing one of the following categories: content-specific vocabulary (blue), generic academic terms (red), all other words already known to my students (**black**).
3. Be selective in what you color-code. Over-color-coding results in what looks like a rainbow, which has the same effect as statements written in all black.

Why Is This Small Move Significant?

Our world is brightly colored, and our students are used to that. Research indicates that strategically color-coding information improves students acquisition and retrieval (Lamberski & Dwyer, 1983). Students' eyes are drawn to the colored term(s), allowing them to focus specifically on that concept without getting overloaded with all the other words in the statement. The colored terms are now coded in their minds as "notable." Color-coding based upon specific criteria that is known to students also increases their ability to organize new learning. If they know that all new math vocabulary will be in red (compared to all other words in black), students begin to automatically recognize each red word as both "new" and "math vocabulary." When we color-code key vocabulary, it also serves as a visual reminder for us to introduce and teach any new terms. This initial exposure is particularly important for English learners, who benefit from both explicit instruction and multiple exposures to new vocabulary (Calderon et al., 2011).

CLASSROOM EXAMPLE

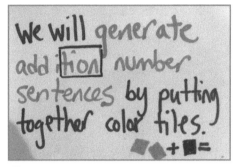

Example

Non-example

Today in Science we will investigate how organism adaptions allow for specific functions by taking guided notes.

Language Focus
I will describe one of my notes using the stem, "_____ ..."

Example

Today in Science we will investigate how organism adaptions allow for specific functions by taking guided notes.

Language Focus
I will describe one of my notes using the stem, "_____ ..."

Non-example

Variations

- If you teach multiple subjects, it is helpful to color-code according to subject. For example, a self-contained teacher might use red butcher paper for her reading bulletin board, and her students might have a red reading journal. In the same class, the bulletin board and journals for math might be blue.

- Code information based upon different criteria than what is described above. An ESL teacher might code all past tense verbs in green, or a social studies teacher might code all names of people and places in purple.

- Annotate the objectives with students.

- Teach students to color-code their own work.

- Instead of using different colors, use other techniques like circling, underlining, highlighting, etc. This is particularly helpful for color-blind students.

Touch to Teach

This straightforward small move is executed when teachers physically touch the resources with which they are teaching. Touching the visual, a real object, the paragraph, the anchor chart, the Promethean board, etc. helps all learners focus on and understand the content more fully. Use your cursor in the same way in a virtual environment.

Challenge a Bad Habit

Providing visual supports to our students is now a common practice. It is rare to teach a lesson without some sort of picture, video clip, or visual example. We plan the visuals ahead of time, and then we explicitly teach using those visuals. After the initial teach (and sometimes even during it), however, the visual supports often become part of the background of a lesson. For example, picture a science teacher highlighting the various layers of the Earth. He displays a diagram that includes the outer core, inner core, mantle, and crust. He teaches about the differences in each layer while he and his students record some notes in their interactive notebooks. Even though the visual is displayed during the entire lesson, neither he nor the students might ever interact with it. Students pay attention to his words and his notes rather than the visual being displayed. They are learning through listening rather than through the combination of listening and seeing.

Implement a Better Habit: *Touch to Teach*

1. Plan visual supports for each lesson.
2. Display the visuals throughout the lesson.
3. Touch (or track with your cursor) the visual whenever you mention it throughout the lesson.
4. Whenever you refer back to that same content (in future lessons, during small-group instruction, or when working with an individual student), touch or point to any available visual supports.

Why Is This Small Move Significant?

Showing a picture on its own is not enough. Without proper explanation and interaction, that visual may be misinterpreted, oversimplified, or completely unnoticed (Davis Bowman, 2018). When we consistently interact with the visual supports in the room, however, we are helping students develop accurate and deep understanding of concepts and increasing their ability to recall such content in future lessons. Touching a visual support while teaching it makes an immediate connection for students. Humans remember pictures more easily than words (Brown et al., 2014). Cueing the picture by touching it provides a direct connection for students (especially those who might be struggling with the academic language of the lesson) to fully focus on what is being communicated and remember it. Interacting with our visuals also increases engagement. One group of researchers found that students' gaze on the teacher lasted 44.9 percent longer when the teacher gestured than when he did not (Araya et al., 2016).

CLASSROOM EXAMPLE

Mr. Mejias is beginning a lesson on the various layers of the Earth. He displays a diagram that shows the inner core, outer core, mantle, and crust.

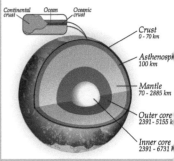

"Today we are going to learn about the structure of the Earth *(drawing an imaginary line around the circumference of the Earth on the diagram)*. The Earth consists of four *(holding up four fingers)* main layers: the crust *(touching the crust)*, the mantle *(touching the mantle),* the outer core (touching the outer core), and the inner core *(touching the inner core)*. Each of these layers has its own unique characteristics.

Let's start with the crust *(touching the crust)*. The crust is where we live *(spreading arms to indicate everyone in the classroom)*. It is the thin outer layer that is anywhere from three to twenty-five miles deep. It is made up of solid rock and minerals like these *(touching the exact part of the crust in the diagram that shows rocks)*. On your graphic organizer, let's jot down some notes about the crust."

Mr. Mejias continues the mini-lesson with the other three layers, continuing to periodically touch the diagram as he discusses the layers. The following day he begins class by saying:

"Yesterday we learned about the different layers of the Earth *(putting his hand on the diagram and making a circular motion)*. I'd like for you and your table to discuss everything you remember learning about the Earth's layers *(pointing to the diagram)* and feel free to use your notes *(holding up his interactive notebook)*."

After the table discussions, he solicits responses from his students. As he listens, he goes back to the diagram to touch the part that represents what each student is explaining.

Variations

- Use total physical response (TPR) as an alternative to print or technology-based visual supports (Gonzalez, 2019). TPR occurs when the teacher connects language with movement, such as a gesture.
- Use a laser pointer, a wand, a stick, etc.
- Encourage students to continue to focus on the visuals and resources around the room by saying things like: "I see a picture of exactly what I am talking about right now. Can you find it?" or "There is one more way to solve this problem. Everyone, look at the anchor charts on the math wall. Which one can help us?"

Tell a Story

In this small move, teachers use a quick story to illustrate the concept being taught.

Challenge a Bad Habit

During the spring semester of a school year, I was telling my class about how my dog figured out how to open the lid to our new kitchen trash can even though it was advertised as "dog proof." One of my students, Jonathan, muttered to himself, "Thought you learned your lesson with the watermelon slicer." Confused, I asked him what he was talking about, and he replied, "When we did that thing at the beginning of the year, and you said you love watermelon but not cutting it. You bought one of those 'as seen on TV' watermelon slicers that makes it look so easy, but you said it didn't work. You told us that maybe one of us could invent one for you that works. I'm just surprised you fell for the 'dog proof' label." I agreed, but I was thinking, "How in the world did he remember that?! I talked about that way back on the second day of school." My next thought about Jonathan (who really struggled in my writing class) was, "How on earth can he remember what I said about watermelon eight months ago, but he can't remember how to create a strong thesis statement even though we've been over it every week for the last eight months?" Then it clicked. He remembered the story. Unfortunately, my watermelon story was unrelated to any of my writing standards, and conversely, one of my most important standards (how to write a strong thesis) never had a story attached to it.

Implement a Better Habit: *Tell a Story*

1. Think about the standard being taught.
2. Create or find a quick story that will help students remember the standard.
3. Tell the story, and explicitly link it to the standard being taught.

Why Is This Small Move Significant?

In doing research for this book, I read a great deal of blog posts, research articles, and books pertaining to the importance of habits. Interestingly, almost every chapter of every book I read about habits began in the same way. Even though these books are filled with references to scientific studies, the chapters all begin with a story. They include tales of how a woman completely changed her life; how a father got his son to eat vegetables; how a company dramatically increased its profits with a small change, etc. Why did these authors begin with so many stories? The story is the hook. The story captures our interest, and the story is what we want to hear. Often I only remember the information because I remember the "lesson" from the story, not because I remember the explanation of the idea or the research behind it. According to Johassen & Hernandez-Serrano (2002), brain scans reveal that stories stimulate and engage the human brain, helping the speaker (the teacher) connect to the audience (the students). For example, in math, the researchers say, if we can anchor a way to solve a problem with a memorable story, students are more likely to remember the problem solving method associated with that story. In addition to building a connection, stories can also be used to create order to curriculum that might otherwise be disjointed. One study showed that experienced teachers do this intuitively (Gudmundsdottir, 1995). Stories also provide a way to connect to what might otherwise be foreign and unfamiliar content. Imagine students who have never been exposed to musical instruments or their classifications before. Their music teacher can offer them a way to connect to those unknown classifications by telling a story. She may use animals (each representing an instrument group) as the main characters, which is something she knows her students can connect to.

CLASSROOM EXAMPLE

My colleague Valentina Gonzalez, a former elementary teacher, shared how she can use one story to connect to two different content areas, writing and science.

WRITING LESSON: HOW TO THINK OF AN IDEA YOU CAN WRITE ABOUT

TEACHER: Writers, one day, I was sitting in my living room watching a movie with my kids when all of a sudden, we heard a strange noise in the garage. We all looked at one another, and I decided to go check it out. I slowly opened the door just a crack. And there in the corner of the garage lay a tiny green hummingbird all wrapped up in plastic netting. It was trapped! The hummingbird was barely moving now and I could tell it needed help. We carefully removed the netting but the bird lay there lifeless. My son and daughter wanted to save it, so they quickly ran and grabbed a bottle cap, some water, and some sugar. We mixed the water and sugar and placed it in the tiny cap. I dropped a small amount on the bird's beak.

All of a sudden, his beak opened, and he began to drink the sugary water. We watched as his small chest went up and down, and then he lifted his body and spread his wings, and off he flew out into the sky. We smiled at each other, and I thought to myself, "It's good to help even the tiniest creatures."

Writers, this is a real story that happened to me long ago. It's a small moment in my life, but it's a story that I can write about as an author. Think about your memories and all the stories from your own life that stand out. You can write about any one of those tiny moments too.

SCIENCE LESSON: THE BASIC NEEDS OF LIVING THINGS

TEACHER: Students, do you remember the story I shared with you about the hummingbird that was trapped in my garage? He could barely move, and even when we removed the netting, he just laid there. After we fed it a few drops of sugar water, he lifted his body and flew out into the sky.

Well, that little hummingbird is a living thing. Living things need food, air, water, and shelter to survive. These are basic needs. The hummingbird needed our help to meet its need for both water and sugar for energy. So, let's think about this. We are living things too; we need food, air, water, and shelter. What is another living thing that needs food, air, water, and shelter to survive? Turn to your partner and share using this sentence stem: "_____ is a living thing because it needs ____, ____, ____, and ____ to survive."

Variations

- Create analogies.
- Capitalize on the vast bank of stories available online (YouTube videos, etc.).
- Create slides or visuals to accompany your story.
- Ask students to write or share any related stories they know.
- Use mnemonic devices.

SMALL MOVE 4.6
Timer

In this small move, the teacher uses a timer and cues students with "time checks" in order to maintain appropriate pacing within a given task or lesson.

Challenge a Bad Habit

Eavesdrop on almost any conversation, and you'll hear mention of timing.

I ran out of time today, but I'll work on it tomorrow.

Either he had a girlfriend or I was dating someone ... our timing was never right.

Hurry, and get your backpack! We need to leave in three minutes.

It's about time! I'm so happy for you!

Our lives revolve around time; minute to minute, day to day, and year to year. Do you ever wonder where the time goes? I have that reflection often in both small moments (How are we late again?!) and in big moments (How is it possible that I have teenage daughters? It seems like just yesterday I was buckling them into car seats). Have you ever grossly underestimated the amount of time a given task takes? I am reminded of a story my sister-in-law told me about her bright idea for an afternoon activity with her two preschoolers: making necklaces. After six trips to the craft store over five days, she finally had some homemade beaded necklaces. They didn't look like what she had envisioned, but they certainly had character.

We all get bogged down in tasks that drain our time. Think laundry. Think talking to customer service about your cell phone bill. Think almost any home project known to man. Time is a huge factor in all that we do, and it can become a tremendous stressor if we do not manage it properly. This rings true in the classroom as well. I've never met a teacher who feels like he has enough time. I always joke that I would start out each year already two weeks behind in my pacing guide. There were countless weeks when I didn't have to write the following week's lesson plans because I was so far behind in the current week's plans that they just carried over. Interestingly, I was also the teacher who often gave students "free time" once they finished their work. On many days if you walked by my classroom five minutes before the end of the period, you'd see kids lining up and socializing as they were listening for the bell. The singular small move that both minimized my falling behind and helped me maximize every instructional minute was the use of a timer. Without the timer I was basing instructional decisions on my perception of time, which was generally inaccurate. With the timer I was basing the same decisions on actual time, and more importantly, making adjustments based on the outcomes of those decisions.

Implement a Better Habit: *Timer*

1. Before beginning a task (activity, assignment, lecture, etc.) estimate how long it will take.
2. Set a timer for that amount of time, and begin.
3. Depending on the length of the task, give "time checks" to the class (e.g., "We have about two more minutes left before we will check our warm-up").
4. When the timer goes off, evaluate whether the task is complete and/or how much more time you'll give for the task. You might want to note if the task took significantly longer or shorter than originally estimated, so you can adjust future instruction accordingly.

Why Is This Small Move Significant?

In the beginning, using a timer is very helpful to build awareness of how much time tasks actually take. For example, a teacher might tell her class "I'll give you two minutes to brainstorm ideas with your partner, and then we will begin writing our plan." Without the timer, often the "two minutes" turns into six minutes as the teacher monitors and listens in to multiple partnerships' conversations. With the aid of the timer, the teacher in the above situation will become aware of exactly how long two minutes is because the alarm will cue her.

Timers also increase focus for both students and teachers. In his book, *15 Secrets Successful People Know About Time Management*, Kevin Kruse (2015) highlights several best-selling authors and bloggers who utilize timers to increase productivity. He uses Franceso Cirillo's "pomodoro technique," which originated in the 1980s. This method

"involves setting a timer for 25 minutes, devoting your full attention to a single task, and then taking a five minute break before repeating the cycle" (Kruse, 2015). While the 25/5 ratio is probably not applicable to all classroom activities, we certainly can reap the same benefits from asking students to fully focus on a task for a specific amount of time. This is effectively "chunking" learning for students into more palatable pieces.

Sometimes using a timer is viewed as "rushing" students. It is important to note that the amount of time we give is completely adjustable. If it goes off and the class needs more time, we can give more time. If I give the class too much time, I can stop them before the timer goes off and begin another task. Providing time checks or "keeping students apprised of the time left for an activity" is a prominent characteristic of effective teaching and learning (Wong et al., 2012, p. 62). In fact, the more we adjust the time, the more effective we will become at estimating the time needed for various tasks.

Consistently using a timer dramatically increases both our time management skills and our students'. When I know how much time I have for a given task and can monitor that throughout the task, it helps me to speed up and slow down in the right places. Our students can also make adjustments to their efforts based upon the timer, making them responsible for structuring their time. Incorporating timers on a regular basis can also create an increased sense of urgency, which is a positive change for some students, especially those who are prone to distraction.

CLASSROOM EXAMPLE

 KINDERGARTEN TEACHER: Good morning, boys and girls. I like how each of you came quickly to the carpet when your table was called. We are now going to begin our morning message. I'm going to set my timer for 10 minutes because that is how long I think it is going to take. *(Ten minutes later the teacher isn't quite finished.)* That was our timer. We are going to add two more minutes so that we can finish this last sentence.

 6TH GRADE TEACHER: I think we are all ready to start our research. I am going to set the timer for 20 minutes. Remember you can work on any of the tasks listed in your Google doc. I'll give you a three-minute warning as well, so you can get to a good stopping point.

 11TH GRADE TEACHER: Check in with your tablemates for one final minute. Make sure each of you has something to share with the class. *(Starts timer for one minute.)*

Variations

- Ask students during "time checks" if they need more or less time. Asking for them to show the number of minutes (zero to five) they need by holding up the respective number of fingers is an effective way to do this. When working in a virtual environment, ask students to type the number of minutes needed into the chat.

- Over time, ask students to estimate the amount of time they will need for the task, allowing them to further practice time management skills.

- Take care to give an appropriate quantity of time cues. Too many cues can break student concentration and communicate a rushed culture. Not giving enough time cues might allow students to lose focus and never regain it.

Fewest Words Possible

In this small move, teachers speak with precision, using the fewest words possible.

Challenge a Bad Habit

Have you ever filmed yourself teaching? If not, I highly recommend it for a number of reasons. Of particular importance is to notice exactly how much you talk during a lesson. In my case it is always a lot more than I think. Here are some of the reasons that I repeat myself or "overtalk" a topic. See if you can relate to any of them.

- Some students aren't paying close attention, so I repeat what I am saying using stronger inflection and extended pauses to try to catch their attention.

- My first explanation didn't quite hit the mark. My students seem a little confused, so I try to explain it in another way. If that doesn't work, I may try a third or fourth way.

- I am about to transition students to working collaboratively or on their own, and I want to make sure they know exactly what to do. I give them directions and then give an abundance of reminders about what I expect to see and not see.

- I think that what I am teaching in that moment is the most valuable part of the lesson, so I repeat it (sometimes quite a few times) to convey its importance.

- I love the standard that I am teaching right now, so I go on and on about it, sharing my passion with long explanations, several stories, and many examples.

No matter the reason, when I talk too much, student learning diminishes.

Implement a Better Habit:
Fewest Words Possible

1. Before you begin giving an explanation, directions, or modeling, think, "What is the most precise way to explain this?"
2. As you speak, be mindful of using the fewest words possible.
3. If you feel the need to repeat or rephrase, instead ask students to repeat or rephrase to a partner. If they are successful, move on. If not, succinctly reteach to clear up their confusion.

Why Is This Small Move Significant?

Have you ever described someone as "a man of few words"? I have a good friend, Bill, who is like that. He is thoughtful, observant, and introverted. A mutual friend said, "It's like he thinks he only has a certain number of words he can use before he dies, and he doesn't want to run out." The thing is, Bill doesn't speak unless he has something of value to say. Because of this, when he speaks, we all listen. As teachers, we can learn from people who use words wisely. When we speak in class, we want our students to listen. Being precise and intentional in our delivery increases our students' ability to focus on our words and process what is being taught. The "less is more" approach is equally important as we facilitate student conversations. Often we interrupt or change the direction of the conversation before students have fully developed their own thinking (Jang & Stecklein, 2011).

CLASSROOM EXAMPLE

Non-example

We are about to get into our research groups. You are going to have 20 minutes to work today. Remember your goal is to identify at least three long-term effects of the environmental problem you selected. All of the topics are right up here on the board. If you forgot which one you picked, look up here. They are all listed right here. When you start, keep your voice level in mind, and I expect to see everyone collaborating. Don't forget that the list of websites is in your Google doc. Use those as your starting point. Oh and yesterday I saw several of you just copy and paste information into your presentation. I do not want to see that. Your presentation should be in your own words, so please do not cut and paste. I'll be walking around to help anyone who might need it. I really want you guys focused today because we only have one more day to work before we start presenting. Each of you will have to present, and so today is your day to discover all of the effects you can. Make good use of your time, and stay on task. Any questions? None?
Ok, get started.

Example

For the next 20 minutes, you and your group will research the long-term effects of the environmental problem you selected. Use the websites on the Google Doc to get started. Your goal is to find at least three long-term effects. Show me with your left hand, on a scale of one to five, how well you understand. Ok, I see mostly fours and fives. You know my expectations.
Let's get started.

Variations

- Create slides for content and directions. Display them as a reference for students.
- Rather than repeating yourself, ask students to repeat what you just said.
- Regularly record portions of your lessons and review them, analyzing how you can be more direct or succinct in your delivery.

Walk With Intention

Walk With Intention is a small move for how to move, literally, around your classroom. Rather than making the "usual loop" to check in on students, assess where your support might be most needed, and deliberately move to that student.

Challenge a Bad Habit

At the end of a training a few years ago, I received this comment on an exit slip from one of the teachers: "I really wish you would teach to the entire room. You must be left handed because you taught almost the whole day from the left side of the room. The back right was totally left out even when you 'walked' the room." My first thought was, "What a strange thing to notice," but it certainly gave me pause. It wasn't a strange thing for the participant who felt left out to notice. It was glaring to her. Regardless of your dominant hand, this is a common occurrence in most classrooms. When we "walk the room" as students are working or collaborating, we often follow the same pattern or loop. I think the unspoken goal is to monitor and check in on each student, but the result in reality is that we often only have time to monitor and check in on the first few students in our path. This means that the first couple of tables of students receive a disproportionately high amount of support compared to the other tables. Additionally, those students weren't selected for any reason other than they are at the beginning of our path. It is likely that some students who would benefit most from

our support are further along on the path and therefore consistently left out. Similar situations occur even in a virtual environment. Teachers often "check in" on break out rooms in numerical order, with room 1 always getting support and room 6 possibly getting missed. Even with asynchronous work, a teacher might look at assignments in alphabetical order or in the order they are received, neither of which might be the most effective order with regards to supporting students who might be struggling.

Implement a Better Habit:
Walk With Intention

1. Before moving anywhere,* scan your class. Look at each student.
2. Determine who would benefit most from your support.
3. Walk to that student or group and provide support.
4. Repeat steps one through three.

Even though you aren't physically moving in a virtual space, the steps are the same with regard to looking at student work or checking in on collaborative tasks.

Why Is This Small Move Significant?

Walking with intention makes you more effective. Moving to a specific student rather than "covering" the room is a way of differentiating instruction. The findings in a review of research about classroom monitoring show that the most effective teachers have systematic procedures for supervising and encouraging students while they work (Cotton, 1988). This small move is the systematic procedure: scan for the next "hot spot," and then walk to it. The most effective teachers also give extra time and attention to students they believe need extra help (Cotton, 1988). Walking with intention might result in spending a large amount of time with a small number of students, but those are the students who need it most, so it is time well spent.

CLASSROOM EXAMPLE

Look at the following classroom maps and the map key:

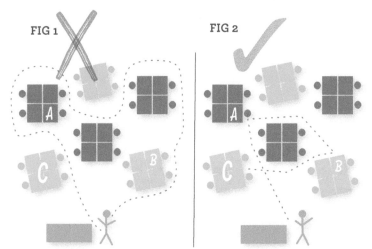

FIG 1   FIG 2

MAP KEY

Student A - Johnny, who is not a self-starter.

Student B - Serena, who just returned from an intervention class and missed THE DIRECTIONS FOR THE ASSIGNMENT. She is also sitting next to Alicia, who really struggles academically.

Student C - This table has four students, all of which are hard working, competitive, and very extroverted.

Look carefully at both figures. Can you see why *Walking With Intention* (Figure 2) is so much more powerful than just "making the loop" (Figure 1)? In Figure 1, the teacher may spend the first two to five minutes at a table where they really don't need any help. When she gets to Johnny, he finally gets started but has wasted the first five minutes of work time. By the time she makes her way to Serena, the work time is almost finished, but Serena was never able to begin.

In Figure 2, the teacher walks with intention. First, she gets Johnny started immediately, and then she scans the class. Next she explains the directions to Serena, which also helps Alicia, who benefits from repeated instructions. She spends another minute with them because Alicia has a question. When she scans the class now, she sees that three of the students at Table 3 are off task, probably because they are finished, so she heads to them.

Figures 3 and 4 represent the same comparison if this were a virtual classroom where the same students are collaborating with each other.

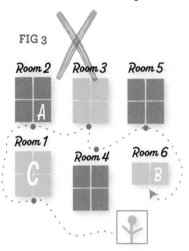

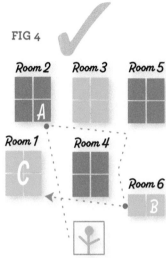

Teacher checks on students in breakout rooms in numerical order:

Breakout Room 1.....1st

Breakout Room 2.....2nd

Breakout Room 3.....3rd

Teacher checks on students in breakout rooms with intention:

Breakout Room 2......1st

Breakout Room 6......2nd

Breakout Room 1......3rd

Variations

• The same principle applies when teachers have students "come to the carpet" for instruction. Sometimes we are unable to move out of our chair because students are so close in proximity to us. When this happens we end up listening to and calling on those who are right by us, leaving other students out. When students are all seated on the floor, be sure to position them in a way where you can get up from your chair and reach any student in the group.

• Have a "Top 5" list in your head of students who consistently need your help. One year a student named Mateo was first in my path because he had a hard time beginning his work. He would sit and stare off into space until someone made sure he had a pencil in his hand and individually encouraged him to begin by touching the assignment and asking him to write his name on his paper. My investment of 10 seconds with him at the very beginning of my monitoring of the class resulted in a dramatic increase in his productivity. He was able to think more and achieve more because of my small move.

School Wide Implementation of *Small Moves*

As with any new training, resource, or school initiative, the common goal is for all teachers to implement the new ideas with fidelity. This is often a challenging task to accomplish. As you have learned in this book, the small moves are not enough. They must become habits. In other words, we cannot just give teachers a training about the moves and expect full implementation. We also have to think about how to support everyone turning those small moves into habits. Just like we give students multiple exposures to new standards, with many opportunities to practice and apply their learning, we must provide teachers with ongoing support as well.

As you think about using this resource to create systemic change, either for your department, your campus, or your district, I encourage you to think about these two questions: What will training look like? What will ongoing support look like? There is no one perfect path for improvement. In most cases, successful schools are using a combination of many of the ideas below.

What will training look like?
- Initial training with all staff focusing on entire book
- Training broken down by content areas
- Training broken down by type of move (talk more, think more, and achieve more)
- Campus book study
- Mini sessions focusing on 1-3 moves each month

What will ongoing support look like?
- Full lesson observation and coaching cycles
- Short campus "walk throughs" to collect data followed by customized mini sessions
- Spotlight 1-3 small moves in PLCs and staff meetings
- Peer to peer observations/Learning walks
- Video record examples and share in common space

On the following page you will find a template that any observer can use to assess implementation. The goal of this form is to help an observer document specific data tied to whichever small moves are the focus of the observation. Unlike many observation tools that allow observers to "click a box" or mark yes or no, data in this case will likely be anecdotal and require the observer to record details. The more precise the information, the more useful it will be when sharing it with the teacher who was observed.

You may have heard the phrases "measure what you treasure" or "inspect what you expect." At the heart of both of these sayings is accountability. We need tools for assessing what is actually happening in classrooms. When using this (or any) observational tool, it is critical to identify who is responsible for measuring implementation. This might be an administrator, a coach or department chair, or ideally, a school leadership team. This form can help you as you consider how to create systemic change by answering the question "how will we measure implementation?"

SMALL MOVES OBSERVATION FORM

Name: _____ Date: _____ Grade/Subject: _____

Small Move	Evidence of Implementation	Growth Opportunities	Comments

Connections to
ELD Standards

While teachers forming these small moves into habits can benefit ALL students, they are particularly supportive to multilingual
learners (MLs). Teachers of MLs are not only responsible for teaching content area standards, such as Common Core State Standards
(CCSS) or Texas Essential Knowledge and Skills (TEKS), but also
English language development (ELD) standards. Many states use the
WIDA Framework or ELPA21 as guidance for how to develop English
language proficiency. In Texas, where I live, we use the English
Language Proficiency Standards (ELPS).

All ELD standards are in place to ensure that teachers of MLs are able
to successfully support students who are learning both content and
language simultaneously. Each of the small moves included in this
resource either directly or indirectly increase a teacher's ability to
achieve this. In the charts below, you will see how each small move is
connected to both the WIDA and the ELPS framework.

WIDA CONNECTIONS TO SMALL MOVES

WIDA Guiding Principles of Language Development (2019)	Small Moves that Support the Guiding Principle
1. Multilingual learners' languages and **cultures are valuable resources** to be leveraged for schooling and classroom life; leveraging these assets and challenging biases **help develop multilingual learners' independence and encourage their agency** in learning.	• Prep the Speaker • Public Success
2. Multilingual learners' development of multiple languages enhances their knowledge and cultural bases, their intellectual capacities, and **their flexibility in language use.**	• Prove It • Solo Sandwich • Anyone's Idea
3. Multilingual learners' language development and learning occur over time through **meaningful engagement in activities** that are valued in their homes, schools, and communities.	• Stop Fishing • Pronounce, Predict, Paraphrase • Timer
4. Multilingual learners' **language, social-emotional, and cognitive development are interrelated processes** that contribute to their success in school and beyond.	• Public Success • Plus Minus • Smile • Tell a Story
5. Multilingual learners use and develop language when opportunities for learning take into account their **individual experiences, characteristics**, abilities, and levels of language proficiency.	• Package and Parrot • Fewest Words Possible
6. Multilingual learners use and develop language through activities which intentionally integrate **multiple modalities**, including oral, written, visual, and kinesthetic modes of communication.	• Target the Talk • Touch to Teach • Color-Code • Walk With Intention
7. Multilingual learners use and develop language **to interpret and access information**, ideas, and concepts from a variety of sources, including real-life objects, models, representations, and multimodal texts.	• Set a Purpose • Listen For… • Non-Example
8. Multilingual learners draw on their **metacognitive, metalinguistic, and metacultural awareness** to develop effectiveness in language use.	• Prove It • Accurate Answer
9. Multilingual learners use their **full linguistic repertoire**, including translanguaging practices, to enrich their language development and learning.	• Appointed Roles • Pick a Number
10. Multilingual learners use and develop language **to interpret and present different perspectives**, build awareness of relationships, and affirm their identities.	• Anyone's Idea • Prep the Speaker • Solo Sandwich

Source: https://wida.wisc.edu/sites/default/files/resource/WIDA-ELD-Standards-Framework-2020.pdf
Emphasis is the author's.

ELPS CONNECTIONS TO SMALL MOVES

English Language Proficiency Standards (ELPS) Cross-curricular language acquisition essential knowledge and skills	Small Moves that support the ELPS
1. Learning Strategies The ELL uses language learning strategies to develop an awareness of his or her own learning processes in all content areas.	• Appointed Roles • Plus Minus • TImer • Prep the Speaker • Color-Code • Touch to Teach • Smile • Public Success • Walk With Intention
2. Listening The ELL listens to a variety of speakers including teachers, peers, and electronic media to gain an increasing level of comprehension of newly acquired language in all content areas.	• Anyone's Idea • Listen For... • Stop Fishing • Tell a Story • Fewest Words Possible • Accurate Answer
3. Speaking The ELL speaks in a variety of modes for a variety of purposes with an awareness of different language registers (formal/informal) using vocabulary with increasing fluency and accuracy in language arts and all content areas.	• Package and Parrot • Target the Talk • Pronounce, Predict, Paraphrase • Prove It • Pick a Number
4. Reading The ELL reads a variety of texts for a variety of purposes with an increasing level of comprehension in all content areas.	• Set a Purpose
5. Writing The ELL writes in a variety of forms with increasing accuracy to effectively address a specific purpose and audience in all content areas.	• Solo Sandwich • Non-Example

Source: https://tea.texas.gov/sites/default/files/ch074a.pdf

ELPA 21 Connections to Small Moves

ELP Standard	Small Moves that support the ELP Standard
1. construct meaning from oral presentations and literary and informational text through grade-appropriate listening, reading, and viewing	• **Listen For...** • **Set a Purpose**
2. participate in grade-appropriate oral and written exchanges of information, ideas, and analyses, responding to peer, audience, or reader comments and questions	• **Target the Talk** • **Prep the Speaker** • **Anyone's Idea** • **Plus Minus**
3. speak and write about grade-appropriate complex literary and informational texts and topics	• **Package and Parrot** • **Target the Talk** • **Appointed Roles**
4. construct grade-appropriate oral and written claims and support them with reasoning and evidence	• **Prove It** • **Solo Sandwich** • **Pick a Number**
5. conduct research and evaluate and communicate findings to answer questions or solve problems	• **Prove It** • **Pick a Number** • **Solo Sandwich**
6. analyze and critique the arguments of others orally and in writing	• **Listen For...** • **Prep the Speaker** • **Plus Minus**
7. adapt language choices to purpose, task, and audience when speaking and writing	• **Pronounce, Predict, Paraphrase** • **Target the Talk**
8. determine the meaning of words and phrases in oral presentations and literary and informational text	• **Pronounce, Predict, Paraphrase** • **Listen For...**
9. create clear and coherent grade-appropriate speech and text	• **Target the Talk** • **Pick a Number** • **Prep the Speaker**
10. make accurate use of standard English to communicate in grade-appropriate speech and writing	• **Accurate Answer** • **Pronounce, Predict, Paraphrase**

Source: https://elpa21.org/wp-content/uploads/2019/03/Final-4_30-ELPA21-Standards_1.pdf

Bibliography

Andrade, H., & Valtcheva, A. (2009). Promoting learning and achievement through self-assessment. *Theory Into Practice, 48*(1), 12-19.

Araya R., Farsani D., & Hernández J. (2016). How to attract students' visual attention. In K. Verbert, M. Sharples, & T. Klobučar (Eds.), *Adaptive and adaptable learning* (pp. 30-41). EC-TEL 2016. Lecture Notes in Computer Science, vol 9891. Springer, Cham. https://link.springer.com/chapter/10.1007/978-3-319-45153-4_3

Ballard, W. (2019, September 25). Teachers make over a thousand decisions each day, and it's exhausting. *Bored Teachers*. https://www.boredteachers.com/classroom-management/teachers-make-four-decisions-per-minute

Beach, R., & Myers, J. (2001). *Inquiry based English instruction: Engaging students in life and literature.* Teachers College Press.

Bingham, G., Holbrook, T., & Meyers, L. (2010). Using self-assessments in elementary classrooms. *The Phi Delta Kappan, 91*(5), 59-61. http://www.jstor.org/stable/27755646

Botzakis, S., Burns, L., & Hall, L. (2014). Literacy reform and common core state standards: Recycling the autonomous model. *Language Arts, 91*(4), 223-235. http://www.jstor.org/stable/24576868

Brown, P., Roediger III, H., & McDaniel, M. (2014). *Make it stick: The science of successful learning.* Harvard University Press.

Calderón, M., Slavin, R., & Sanchez, M. (2011). Effective instruction for English learners. *The Future of Children, 21*(1), 103–127. JSTOR. www.jstor.org/stable/41229013

Cervetti, G., DiPardo, A., & Staley, S. (2014). Entering the conversation: Exploratory talk in middle school science. *The Elementary School Journal, 114*(4), 547-572. doi:10.1086/675638

Cirillo, F. (2018). *The pomodoro technique: The acclaimed time-management system that has transformed how we work.* Penguin Random House.

Clapper, T. (2010). Creating a safe learning environment. *PAILAL Newsletter, 3*(2), 1-6.

Clear, J. (2018). *Atomic habits: An easy & proven way to build good habits & break bad ones.* Penguin Random House.

Cotton, K. (1988). *Monitoring student learning in the classroom.* Northwest Regional Educational Laboratory.

Curtis, C. P. (1997, c1995). *The Watsons go to Birmingham—1963.* Yearling Book.

Davenport, B. (2016). *Sticky habits: How to achieve your goals without quitting and create unbreakable habits starting with 5 minutes a day.* Bold Living Press.

Davis Bowman, J. (2018, June 20). Making the most of visual aids: Three strategies for using visual aids to encourage students to engage more deeply with course content. *Edutopia.* https://www.edutopia.org/article/making-most-visual-aids

Doughty, C., Varela, E. (1998). Communicative focus on form. In C. Doughty & J. Williams (Eds.), Focus on form in classroom second language acquisition (pp. 114-138). Cambridge University Press.

Duhigg, C. (2014). *The power of habit: Why we do what we do in life and business.* Random House.

Ekman, P., & Davidson, R. (1993). Voluntary smiling changes regional brain activity. *Psychological Science, 4*(5), 342-345.

Escalante, L. B. (2018). *Motivating ELLs: 27 activities to inspire and engage students.* Seidlitz Education.

Ferlazzo, L., & Hull Sypnieski, K. (2018). *The ELL teacher's toolbox: Hundreds of practical ideas to support your students.* Jossey-Bass.

Frey, N., Fisher, D., & Nelson, J. (2013). Todo tiene que ver con lo que se habla: It's all about the talk. *The Phi Delta Kappan, 94*(6), 8-13. http://www.jstor.org/stable/23611743

Gallo, C. (2014). *Talk like TED: The 9 public-speaking secrets of the world's top minds.* St. Martin's Griffin.

Gladwell, M. (2008). *Outliers: The story of success.* Little, Brown and Company.

Gonzalez, V. (2019, May 8). Total physical response: Learning through action. *Seidlitz Education.* https://seidlitzblog.org/2019/05/08/total-physical-response-learning-through-action/#more-137

Guccione, L. (2011). Integrating literacy and inquiry for English learners. *The Reading Teacher, 64*(8), 567-577.

Gudmundsdottir, S. (1995). The narrative nature of pedagogical content knowledge. In H. McEwan & K. Egan (Eds.), *Narrative in teaching, learning, and research.* Teachers College Press.

Guise, S. (2013). *Mini habits: Smaller habits, bigger results.* CreateSpace Publishing.

Halwani, N. (2017). Visual aids and multi-media in second language acquisition. *English Language Teaching, 10*(6), 53-59.

Haneda, M. & Wells, G. (2008). Learning an additional language through dialogic inquiry. *Language and Education, 22*(2), 114-136.

Havranek, G. (2002). When is corrective feedback most likely to succeed? *International Journal of Education Research, 37*, 255-270.

Helmke, A. & Schrader, F. W. (1988). Successful student practice during seatwork: Efficient management and active supervision not enough. *The Journal of Educational Research, 82*(2), 70-76.

Hebert, C. R. (2007). *Catch a falling reader.* Corwin Press.

Jang, J., & Stecklein, J. (2011). Methods & strategies: Less talk but better teacher feedback: Using redirects to improve student-to-student discussions. *Science and Children, 48*(9), 80-83. http://www.jstor.org/stable/43175824

Jensen, E. (2008). *Brain-based learning: A new paradigm of teaching*. Sage Publications.

Johnson, E. (2011). Developing listening skills through peer interaction. *Music Educators Journal, 98*(2), 49-54. http://www.jstor.org/stable/41433247

Jonassen, D. H., & Hernandez-Serrano, J. (2002). Case-based reasoning and instructional design: Using stories to support problem solving. *Educational Technology Research and Development, 50*(2), 65-77.

Ketch, A. (2005). Conversation: The comprehension connection. *The Reading Teacher, 59*(1), 8-13. www.jstor.org/stable/20204313

Kruse, K. (2015). *15 secrets successful people know about time management: Summary*. Quick Reads. https://www.quickread.com/book-summary/15-secrets-successful-people-know-about-time-management-59

Lamberski, R. J., & Dwyer, F. M. (1983). The instructional effect of coding (color and black and white) on information acquisition and retrieval. *ECTJ, 31*(1), 9-21.

Lawson, M., & Lawson, H. (2013). New conceptual frameworks for student engagement research, policy, and practice. *Review of Educational Research, 83*(3), 432-479. http://www.jstor.org/stable/24434165

Lemov, D., Woolawy, E., & Yezzi, K. (2012). *Practice perfect: 42 rules for getting better at getting better*. Jossey-Bass.

National Research Council & Institute of Medicine. (2004). *Engaging schools: Fostering high school students' motivation to learn*. National Academies Press.

Marzano, R., Pickering, D., & Pollock, J. (2001). *Classroom instruction that works: Research based strategies for increasing student achievement*. Pearson.

Matis, A., & Seidlitz, J. (2018). *7 steps to a language-rich, interactive foreign language classroom: Strategies for teachers of languages other than English (LOTE)*. Seidlitz Education.

Morgan, D. N., Williams, J. L., Clark, B., Hatteberg, S., Marek Hauptman, G., Kozel, C., & Paris, J. (2013). Guiding readers in the middle grades: Teachers can use guided reading strategies to help students achieve CCSS for literacy. *Middle School Journal, 44*(3), 16–24. JSTOR. www.jstor.org/stable/41763125

Motley, N. (2016). *Talk, read, talk, write: A practical routine for learning in all content areas (K-12)*. 2nd Ed. Seidlitz Education.

Motley, N. (2019, May 1). Target the talk. *Seidlitz Education*. https://seidlitzblog.org/2019/05/01/target-the-talk

move. (2019). In *Merriam-Webster.com*. https://www.merriam-webster.com/dictionary/move

Munns, G., & Woodard, H. (2006). Student engagement and student self-assessment: The REAL framework. *Assessment in Education, 13*(2), 193-213.

Prince, M., & Felder, R. (2007, February 15). The many faces of inductive teaching and learning. *NSTA WebNews Digest.* https://my.nsta.org/resource/?id=10.2505/4/jcst07_036_05_14

Ritchhart, R., Church, M., & Morrison, K. (2011). *Making thinking visible: How to promote engagement, understanding, and independence for all learners.* Jossey-Bass.

Routman, R. (2000). *Conversations: Strategies for teaching, learning, and evaluating.* Heinemann.

Rubin, G. (2015). *Better than before: What I learned about making and breaking habits-to sleep more, quit sugar, procrastinate less, and generally build a happier life.* Broadway Books.

Schmoker, M. (2006). *Results now.* Association for Supervision and Curriculum Development.

Schultz, K. (2012). The role of silence in teaching and learning. *Educational Horizons, 91*(2), 22-25. http://www.jstor.org/stable/42927162

Scott, S. J. (2014). *Habit stacking: 97 small life changes that take 5 minutes or less.* Create Space.

Seidlitz, J., & Perryman, B. (2021). *7 steps to a language-rich, interactive classroom.* Seidlitz Education.

Skinner, E. A., & Pitzer, J. R. (2012). Developmental dynamics of student engagement, coping, and everyday resilience. In S. L. Christenson, A. L. Reschley, & C. Wylie (Eds.), *Handbook of research on student engagement,* 21-44. Springer.

Stanford, A., & Henderson, J. (2016). Dissecting student dialogue: Speaking and listening, in the form of collaborative conversation, enhances the depth of students' science knowledge. *Science and Children, 54*(3), 40-46. http://www.jstor.org/stable/24893799

Taylor, S., & Nesheim, D. (2000). Making literacy real for "high-risk" adolescent emerging readers: An innovative application of readers' workshop. *Journal of Adolescent & Adult Literacy, 44*(4), 308-318. http://www.jstor.org/stable/40015344

Wong, H., Wong, R., Rogers, K., & Brooks, A. (2012). Managing your classroom for success. *Science and Children, 49*(9), 60-64. http://www.jstor.org/stable/43747385

Zwiers, J. (2011). Reading is your thing (Even if you're not a reading teacher). *The Reading Teacher, 64*(7), 543-545.

Nancy Motley is a Senior Educational Consultant for Seidlitz Education, specializing in literacy and second language acquisition strategies. For the past decade her work with teachers, schools, and districts has centered around increasing students' success with straight-forward and actionable techniques. She is widely known for her "user-friendly" approach.

Nancy is the author of *Talk, Read, Talk, Write: A practical routine for learning in all content areas (K-12)*, 1st and 2nd editions. This effective resource and teaching routine is transforming classrooms across the nation into literacy dense learning environments. She is also the co-author of *The Diverse Learner Flip Book,* and has developed hundreds of customized professional development modules focused on meeting the needs of multilingual learners, magnifying student engagement, and increasing reading, writing, and communication skills for all students. Nancy's previous educational roles included: classroom teacher, reading specialist, intervention program coordinator, professional development instructor, and curriculum developer.

Because of her dynamic approach to teaching and learning, she was awarded the Alief Independent School District's Teacher of the Year Award in 2003. Her passion for and commitment to education is still just as evident today as she trains and coaches teachers, collaborates with leadership, and creates new educational resources.

She holds a Masters of Arts in Counseling that she uses to help teachers build strong, authentic connections with their students. Nancy lives in Houston, Texas with her husband and two wonderful daughters.

@nancymotleyTRTW

Acknowledgments

To Marshall, Audrey, and Caroline, I love you! I think y'all got the short end of the stick with regards to my career, but no one would ever know. You love me unconditionally and support me without qualification, and for that, I am so tremendously blessed. I could never be the person I am to so many teachers without being so cherished at home.

To John, who would have thought after that silly little "disgruntled participant" simulation in your small office in San Antonio that I would be where I am today? I know I couldn't have conceived it at the time, and as sure as I know that, I also know that you absolutely did conceive it. You had a vision for me and for your company, and I am honored to be part of its realization. Thank you for giving me my wings and for continually showing me new places to fly.

To my Seidlitz team, you are the true embodiment of Proverbs 27:17: "Iron sharpens iron, so one man sharpens another." Your knowledge, your passion, your insights, and your humor propel me forward in this fulfilling but often challenging work we do. Mónica, thank you for blazing this trail with me. To all the other Seidlitz consultants, thank you for allowing me to learn from you every time we meet. Meg, Anna, and Anne Charlotte, just wow! Thank you for transforming my ideas into something so beautiful (and grammatically correct) and yet still maintaining my voice. Michelle, thank you for doing all the things I am terrible at and for doing them with grace and accuracy. Kathy, you are my biggest cheerleader, and I love you for that! Thank you for always being the glue that keeps us together.

To my clients, colleagues, and consultants, who have now also become my friends, thank you for your collaboration and support. A special thank you to Heather Mavel, who through her insightful feedback, made this book tremendously better.

To my favorite people on earth: teachers!! You have the grittiest job there is, and you grind it out everyday. Thank you for showing up, literally and figuratively, for your students. Thank you for the tender care as well as the tough love you show them each day. Thank you for being lifelong learners who are always striving to give your kids the best instruction possible. I can only hope this book will be one small part of that.

SEIDLITZ EDUCATION

BOOK ORDER FORM

Pricing, specifications, and availability subject to change without notice.

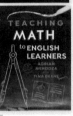

TITLE	PRICE	QTY	TOTAL$
38 Great Academic Language Builders	$24.95		
7 Steps to a Language-Rich Interactive Classroom 2ND ED.	$32.95		
7 Steps To a Language-Rich, Interactive Foreign Language Classroom (LOTE)	$32.95		
Boosting Achievement: Reaching Students with Interrupted or Minimal Education	$26.95		
Content Review & Practice for the TX ESL 154 4TH ED.	$39.95		
Content Review & Practice for the TX Bilingual 164	$39.95		
Content Review & Practice for the TX Spanish 190	$39.95		
Diverse Learner Flip Book 2ND ED.	$29.95		
DIY PD: A Guide to Self-Directed Learning for Teachers of Multilingual Learners NEW!	$29.95		
ELLs in Texas: What Teachers Need to Know 2ND ED.	$34.95		
ELs in Texas: What School Leaders Need to Know 3RD ED.	$34.95		
ELPS Flip Book	$19.95		
English/Spanish Linguistic and Academic Connections	$29.95		
If You Only Knew: Letters from an Immigrant Teacher	$14.99		
Juan José You Are Especial	$9.97		
Mi Cuaderno de Dictado SPANISH	$7.95		
Motivating ELLs: 27 Activities to Inspire & Engage Students	$26.95		
Navigating the ELPS: Using the Standards to Improve Instruction for English Learners	$24.95		
Navigating the ELPS: Math 2ND ED.	$29.95		
Navigating the ELPS: Science	$29.95		
Navigating the ELPS: Social Studies	$29.95		
Navigating the ELPS: Language Arts and Reading	$34.95		
Optimizando el desarrollo de la lectoescritura SPANISH	$39.95		
Pathways to Greatness for ELL Newcomers: A Comprehensive Guide for Schools & Teachers	$32.95		
Portraits of Collaboration	$32.95		
Reading & Writing with English Learners	$29.95		
RTI for ELLs Fold-Out	$16.95		
Sheltered Instruction in Texas: Second Language Acquisition Methods for Teachers of ELs	$29.95		
Small Moves, Big Gains: Teacher Habits that Help Kids To Talk More, Think More, Achieve More	$32.95		
Solved: A Teacher Guide to Making Word Problems Comprehensible	$26.95		
Talk Read Talk Write: A Practical Routine for Learning in All Content Areas K-12 2ND ED.	$32.95		
Teaching Math to English Learners	$24.95		
Teaching Social Studies to ELLs	$24.95		
Teaching Science to English Learners	$24.95		
¡Toma la Palabra! SPANISH	$32.95		
Vocabulary Now! 44 Strategies All Teachers Can Use	$29.95		

HOW TO ORDER

www.seidlitzeducation.com

CALL (210) 315-7119

FAX completed form to (949) 200-4384 with credit card info or attached purchase order

NAME

SHIPPING ADDRESS

CITY   STATE   ZIP

PHONE   EMAIL

Select payment method:

☐ Purchase Order attached
   please make P.O. out to Seidlitz Education

☐ Visa ☐ MasterCard ☐ Discover ☐ AMEX

CARD #

EXPIRES   CVV

SIGNATURE

TAX EXEMPT? please fax a copy of your certificate along with order.

SHIPPING 9% of order total, minimum $14.95
5-7 business days to ship.
If needed sooner please call for rates.

SUBTOTAL $	
DISCOUNT $	
SHIPPING $	
TAX $	
TOTAL $	

Learn more about Seidlitz Education products and professional development.

www.seidlitzeducation.com
(210) 315-7119 | michelle@seidlitzeducation.com
56 Via Regalo, San Clemente, CA 92673

Developing language in every classroom.™

Seidlitz
EDUCATION

REV08/10/22

TITLE	Price	QTY	TOTAL $
Instead Of I Don't Know Poster For the LOTE Classroom 24" x 36"	**3 pack**			
☐ LOTE FRENCH	$29.85		
☐ LOTE SPANISH	$29.85		
☐ LOTE GERMAN	$29.85		
☐ LOTE ARABIC NEW!	$29.85		
☐ LOTE CHINESE NEW!	$29.85		
		TOTAL	$

TITLE	Price	QTY	TOTAL $
Instead Of I Don't Know Poster, 24" x 36"	**3 pack**			
☐ Elementary ENGLISH	$29.85		
☐ Secondary ENGLISH	$29.85		
Instead Of I Don't Know Posters, 11" x 17"| **20 pack**			
☐ Elementary ENGLISH	$40.00		
☐ Secondary ENGLISH	$40.00		
Instead Of I Don't Know Poster, 24" x 36"	**3 pack** Elementary SPANISH	$29.85		
Instead Of I Don't Know Posters, 11" x 17"	**20 pack** Elementary SPANISH	$40.00		
		TOTAL	$

TITLE	Price	QTY	TOTAL $
Academic Language Cards and Activity Booklet, ENGLISH	$19.95		
Academic Language Cards, SPANISH	$9.95		
		TOTAL	$

TITLE	Price	QTY	TOTAL $
Please Speak In Complete Sentences Poster 24" x 36"	**3 pack** ☐ ENGLISH ☐ SPANISH	$29.85		
Please Speak In Complete **Sentences** Posters,11" x 17"	**20 pack** ☐ ENGLISH ☐ SPANISH	$40.00		
		TOTAL	$

TAX EXEMPT? please fax a copy of your certificate along with order.

SHIPPING 9% of order total, minimum $14.95
5-7 business days to ship.
If needed sooner please call for rates.

GRAND TOTAL	$
DISCOUNT	$
SHIPPING	$
TAX	$
FINAL TOTAL	$

HOW TO ORDER

www.seidlitzeducation.com

CALL (210) 315-7119

FAX completed form to (949) 200-4384 with credit card info or attached purchase order

NAME

SHIPPING ADDRESS

CITY   STATE   ZIP

PHONE   EMAIL

Developing language in every classroom.™

Seidlitz EDUCATION

Select payment method:

☐ Purchase Order attached
please make P.O. out to Seidlitz Education

☐ Visa ☐ MasterCard ☐ Discover ☐ AMEX

CARD #

EXPIRES   CVV

SIGNATURE